That Complex Whole

THAT
COMPLEX
WHOLE

*Culture and the Evolution
of Human Behavior*

Lee Cronk, Ph.D.

Texas A&M University

Westview Press
A Member of the Perseus Books Group

Copyright © 1999 by Westview Press, A Member of the Perseus Books Group

Published in 1999 in the United States of America by Westview Press, 5500 Central Avenue, Boulder,
Colorado 80301-2877, and in the United Kingdom by Westview Press, 12 Hid's Copse Road, Cumnor
Hill, Oxford OX2 9JJ

Find us on the World Wide Web at www.westviewpress.com

Library of Congress Cataloging-in-Publication Data
Cronk, Lee
   That complex whole: culture and the evolution of human behavior /
Lee Cronk.
      p.   cm.
   Includes bibliographical references and index.
   ISBN 0-8133-3704-6 (Hardcover).   ISBN 0-8133-3705-4 (pbk.)
   1. Sociobiology.   2. Culture.   3. Human behavior.   I. Title.
GN365.9.C76   1999
304.5—dc21
                                                                                99-28032
                                                                                CIP

10   9   8   7   6   5   4   3   2   1

To Lauren and Cooper

Contents

Preface

This book had its start, in a sense, as a high-school term paper. An assignment in my eleventh grade Basic Composition class was to write a research paper on the career of my choice. I chose to write about being an anthropologist. I still am not sure where I got the idea that I might like to be an anthropologist. Perhaps it was from my family's emphasis on travel and cross-cultural education. Perhaps it was the fascinating knickknacks and beautiful rugs that filled the house of a friend whose father was an anthropologist. Whatever its source, my fascination with behavior and cultural diversity started at an early age, and I devoured the few anthropology books in my local library.

For reasons that also go back to my high-school days of the late 1970s, cultural anthropology, the discipline I love, is in trouble. One of my other great intellectual passions at that time was biology, particularly the story of evolution, and I was understandably thrilled when, in the mid-1970s, these two areas of interest—culture and biology—seemed to be converging. 1975 saw the publication of E. O. Wilson's landmark *Sociobiology: The New Synthesis*, followed closely in 1976 by Richard Dawkins' *The Selfish Gene.*[1] I clearly recall the huge display devoted to Wilson's book at the neighborhood bookstore and excitedly showing a copy of the book to my biology teacher. Dawkins' book was fascinating to me as well, and I headed for college certain that professional cultural anthropologists would share my enthusiasm for these new ideas from evolutionary biology, which promised to shed light on so many issues of importance to them.

I was wrong. What I did not realize at the time was that the discipline of cultural anthropology, along with the rest of the social sciences, had invested many decades in developing its approach to human affairs in isolation from biology. For Wilson, Dawkins, and a few renegade anthropologists suddenly to propose that biology was more important—and, by implication, that culture was less important—than they had thought was shocking, insulting, and even dangerous in the eyes of most cultural anthropologists. One prominent cultural anthropologist, Marshall Sahlins of the University of Chicago, quickly wrote his own little book, *The Use and Abuse of Biology*, in an effort to nip the weed of sociobiology in the bud.[2]

That weed, pruned of some of its youthful excesses, has since grown into a large and vigorous tree. The only problem is, it has mostly grown in someone else's garden. Although the efforts of Sahlins and others did help seal cultural anthropology off from the idea that our species' evolutionary heritage might be relevant to an understanding of our current behavior, it did little to dissuade scientists in other fields from pursuing that heretical notion. The approach is now thriving in such fields as psychology, ethology, linguistics, neuroscience, economics, political science, and even in cultural anthropology's sister subdiscipline, biological anthropology. At the same time that biology has become more and more incorporated into those fields, cultural anthropology has moved in another direction entirely, convinced of the specialness of culture as a subject matter and the distinctiveness of our own species.

Because of its refusal to acknowledge the significance of our species' evolutionary past, cultural anthropology is growing increasingly isolated from and irrelevant to the other sciences as well as from public life and political discourse. More and more often one reads disparaging and condescending accounts of cultural anthropologists' tendency to harp on the overriding significance of culture in human affairs, to the exclusion of all else. For example, someone unfamiliar with cultural anthropology would come away from MIT linguist Steven Pinker's brilliant and best-selling *The Language Instinct* with the impression that my discipline produces nothing but "anthropological canards" and "chestnuts," such as the idea that the Hopi do not have a sense of time or that the Inuit have scores of words for "snow" (neither of which turns out to be true).[3] Frans de Waal, a primatologist at Emory University, recently told a story in *The Chronicle of Higher Education* about a cultural anthropologist who announced at a scholarly meeting on sexuality that people who speak a language that lacks a word for "orgasm" must not be able to experience one, prompting the natural scientists present to circulate "little notes among ourselves with naughty questions such as 'Without a word for "oxygen," can people breathe?'"[4] Richard Dawkins, in one of his more recent books, mentions an anthropologist who insists that a Western scientist's understanding that the moon is a large, rocky sphere about a quarter of a million miles away is no more valid or true than a tribal belief that it is actually a calabash tossed in the sky and hanging there, just out of reach above the treetops.[5] And Lionel Tiger, an anthropologist at Rutgers who, together with his colleague Robin Fox, helped lay the foundation for the approach described in this book, sarcastically writes that "the majority social-construction-of-reality crowd" in anthropology ultimately "may have as much impact on international science as phrenologists" due to the "scientific ludicrousness" and "utter impracticality" of their approach.[6]

Such snide and snickering comments about cultural anthropology are, on the one hand, sad and embarrassing to me as a cultural anthropologist and, on the other, worrisome to me as a proponent of the study of our evolved human nature. While it is true that cultural anthropologists have raised the concept of culture to the level of a fetish, it is also true that no approach to human behavior that ignores culture can last for very long, no matter how productive and insightful it may be in its early years. Those of us who study the evolution of human behavior must find a way to incorporate the culture concept into our approach, and, at a more practical level, our society's social and political discourse is badly in need of an infusion of clear thinking on the issue of culture and its role in shaping human behavior. To accomplish these goals, we need the sophisticated understanding of culture and its variations among human societies that only cultural anthropology can provide. Conversely, for cultural anthropology to continue to be relevant to society in general and to the rest of the social and behavioral sciences, it must cease to develop in isolation from those other fields.

I wish I could claim that this book explains exactly how to accomplish this important goal, but I am afraid that it does not. It does, however, point out some of the major problems we face when trying to create a truly biocultural approach to human affairs and offer some tentative suggestions and possible solutions.

Perhaps the largest stumbling block in developing a truly biocultural approach to human affairs is the confusion surrounding the culture concept itself. Building on the work of cognitive and symbolic anthropologists of the 1950s and 1960s, Chapter 1 presents the argument that to be useful, the culture concept must be whittled down to its most basic element: socially transmitted information. One pitfall of many previous definitions of culture that is crucial to avoid is the inclusion of behavior in the category of culture. The gap between culture and behavior is made obvious by an examination of the many discrepancies that exist between what people say and what they actually do. Separating behavior from the concept of culture allows us to avoid the circularity of explanations of culture in terms of itself and the illusion that all behavior is cultural.

One of the most common objections to the idea that there is such a thing as a common, evolved human nature is the great cultural diversity shown by the world's societies. Chapter 2 examines this diversity and finds that, first, it is not as great as one might imagine; second, what diversity that does exist is not always attributable to culture; and, third, that evidence of a large number of universal characteristics across human societies suggests that a shared, evolved human nature is a significant factor in human affairs.

Another claim often made to fend off biological intrusions into the human sciences is the idea that there is something about humans and their cultures that makes studying them fundamentally different from studying, say, chemicals, plants, or animals. Chapter 3 argues that although no one method may suit all of the sciences and although no science has veto power over any other, the sciences cannot be divided in this way. No true scientific knowledge can exist in isolation from the rest of our scientific knowledge.

The project of linking the information collected by anthropologists about human behavior and cultural diversity with the rest of our scientific knowledge of the universe began in earnest with the sociobiologists of the late 1970s and now continues under such rubrics as evolutionary ecology, evolutionary psychology, and behavioral ecology. Chapter 4 describes some of their major theoretical models and empirical findings on topics like mating, parenting, and social behavior.

This book is not the first attempt to combine an understanding of culture with a concern for our species' evolutionary past. Chapter 5 describes one approach to this problem, commonly known as memetics. It relies on an analogy between genes and cultural traits, or memes, both of which are heritable packages of information. Memeticists have developed a sophisticated suite of models dealing with topics such as how culture is transmitted from person to person and how it interacts with genes to produce human behavior.

Memes are in some ways similar to genes, but they are also sometimes similar to viruses. Like viruses and other pathogens, memes are passed from person to person and may not necessarily be helpful to the people who catch them. But few memes are really like wild flu viruses, developing and spreading without human intervention. Rather, they are much more similar to biological warfare viruses in that they are designed and used by people in their efforts to manipulate one another. They are, in short, the raw material out of which humans fashion the signals they send one another. Chapter 6, which is in many ways the heart of this book, explains how the culture concept can be easily incorporated into a study of humans as evolved organisms by focusing on exactly how people use culture in communication and social manipulation.

Although anthropologists like to think of the culture concept as their own, in actuality it is widely used in other fields, and in recent years especially, it has gained a prominent place in political discourse in the United States and elsewhere. Given the widespread appeal and use of the culture concept, any approach that claims to shed new light on the role of culture in human lives must in some way change not only anthropology but also those wider debates about the role of culture in society. For example, much has been made recently of the doctrines of cultural and moral relativism. On the one hand, this book's argument that culture is essentially a tool people use to manipulate one another implies that it no longer makes sense to sanctify it with the doctrine of cultural relativism. Arguments defending objectionable practices like female genital mutilation on the grounds that they are "cultural" are no more valid than arguments defending behaviors like rape on the grounds that they are "natural." Both sorts of arguments make an unwarranted leap from a description of how things are to a pronouncement about how they ought to be. On the other hand, if, as argued early in this book, culture is not as important a determinant of human behavior and as crucial an element in our social lives as has traditionally been believed by many social scientists and political pundits, then it also does not make sense to treat culture as a political football. Doing so may simply be a way of distracting people, of turning their attention away from the real sources of social problems. Furthermore, some of the sources of those problems may be clarified by taking seriously the idea that we, like all organisms, are products of an evolutionary process that began long, long ago. Like all organisms, we are the products of a process of evolution that occurred in a series of environments that in many ways were quite unlike the environment in which we live today. It is possible that a variety of problems of modern life, ranging from some types of cancer to broad feelings of alienation and loneliness, can be attributed to a mismatch between our ancestral and modern environments. Culture will undoubtedly play a crucial role in helping us deal with these kinds of problems, just as it always has.

Although I will happily take the blame for any shortcomings this book might have, I must share the credit for its strengths with the great many people who helped me with it in big and little ways. Chapter 1 is a more or less direct result of conversations with Kathy Dettwyler, who made me realize that I could not take it for granted that my colleagues would share my belief in the value of an ideational definition of culture. The discussion of animal cultures included in Chapter 1 was first presented at the 1996 annual meetings of the Southwest Comparative Psychology Association in a session organized by Del Thiessen. I originally presented the core argument of Chapter 2 at a conference organized by Brett Cooke of Texas A&M University's Department of

Modern and Classical Languages, and a version of that talk is to be included in a volume edited by Brett Cooke and Frederick Turner.[7] Chapter 3 was inspired by a conversation with Richard Hall, a political scientist at the University of Iowa, who forced me to defend the idea of the unity of scientific knowledge. Some of the ideas in Chapter 3 also owe a great deal to conversations with my archaeologist colleagues here at Texas A&M University, particularly D. Bruce Dickson and David Carlson, and I am grateful to the staff of the American Anthropological Association for providing me with a copy of an old item from *Anthropology Newsletter* that I needed for that chapter. Kristen Hawkes helped me understand a crucial point in Chapter 4. I first presented many of the arguments included in Chapter 6 in a plenary address given to the 1995 annual meeting of the Human Behavior and Evolution Society, and I would like to thank the program chairs for that meeting, John Tooby and Leda Cosmides, for giving me the chance to convince myself that I actually had something significant to say on this topic. Some of the ideas in Chapters 5 and 6 were also present in papers I read at the 1991 annual meetings of the American Sociological Association in a session organized by Joseph Lopreato, at the 1993 annual meetings of the American Association for the Advancement of Science in a session organized by Philip Hefner and William Irons, and at the 1993 annual meetings of the American Anthropological Association in a session organized by Roger Lohmann as well as in an article published in *Evolution and Human Behavior*, on which Martin Daly, Henry Harpending, and an anonymous reviewer made some valuable suggestions. Parts of the argument presented in Chapter 7 were originally part of a column published in *The Sciences*.[8] I would like to thank the folks at Equality Now, Fran Mooney of the Immigration Review Board, and the law firm of Braverman and Linarelli for help in tracking down some information on female genital mutilation and Vaughn M. Bryant, Jr., for helpful feedback on part of that chapter.

Matt Ridley and Robert Wright helped me take my original somewhat hazy plans for a book and turn them into something coherent and marketable. Brett Cooke, William Irons, Beth Leech, Jeffry A. Simpson, and an anonymous reviewer read the entire manuscript, and their comments and suggestions vastly improved the final product. My good friend and colleague D. Bruce Dickson provided me with stimulating discussions of many of the topics covered in this book, several key references, and some outstanding ideas for a title. Karl Yambert at Westview Press deserves my thanks for his enthusiasm and encouragement as well as for all of the hard work he has done on this book from his end of things.

Academics are fond of saying that there is a wonderful synergism between teaching and research, though usually what they have in mind is how a scholar's research can enhance his teaching. This book is an example of how it can also work the other way: Teaching can enhance a scholar's intellectual development, and thus his research. This book simply would not have been written had I not had to deal with many basic issues, like the concept of culture itself, to teach courses on anthropological theory. And so my final thanks go to the many graduate and undergraduate students who, in a variety of classes over the past several years, have challenged me to hone, develop, and clarify my ideas on these topics.

Lee Cronk

1

Righting Culture

Our common culture serves as a kind of immunological system, destroying the values and attitudes promulgated by an adversary culture that can infect our body politic. Should our common culture begin to break down, should its fundamental premises fail to be transmitted to succeeding generations, then we will have reason to worry.

—William Bennett[1]

Culture Wars

Culture, once staid and stale, is now the stuff of vigorous debate. From the left come calls for multicultural education and public recognition and acceptance of diverse moral systems, values, and cultures that exist among the world's peoples and increasingly within our own society. Those on the right, fearful of a creeping moral relativism, counter with demands that English be made the nation's official language, that material that offends them be censored, and that the public schools increase the amount of time they spend on moral instruction.

Ironically, those on both sides share one important characteristic: a deep reverence for the concept of culture, a belief that culture is so fundamental to society and so powerful an influence on behavior that it is very much worth fighting over. To former Reagan administration official William Bennett, for example, the stakes in the debate are clear: "Whoever wins the battle for culture gets to teach the children."[2] This is important to Bennett because he is a believer in the power of culture: "What determines a young person's behavior

in academic, sexual, and social life are his deeply held convictions and beliefs. They determine behavior far more than race, class, economic background, or ethnicity."³ These sorts of concerns have motivated Bennett to
write a series of best-selling books, such as *The Moral Compass, The Book of
Virtues,* and *The Children's Book of Virtues,* intended to teach a variety of core
moral values to the nation's adults and children.⁴ Those books were turned
into an animated television series called *Adventures from the Book of Virtues*
broadcast on some educational stations around the country and even into a
set of plastic toys that were included in children's meals at Wendy's ham-
burger restaurants.

To those on the left, the power of culture is equally clear. Indeed, it is precisely because culture is so powerful, they argue, that we must be extraordinarily tolerant of cultural diversity, even when it leads people to do things we
find repugnant. Just as our culture is the basis for all our values, so are other
people's cultures the basis for their values. All values are equally valid and
stand on equally firm (or shaky) ground. To claim any priority for one's own
moral system, the left argues, reflects an ignorance of the world's amazing cultural diversity and a degree of ethnocentrism that can easily slide into xenophobia, racism, and sexism. All cultures are equally valid and worthy of study
and respect, and, accordingly, many universities and colleges offer courses on
topics like gay and lesbian culture and the appreciation of rock 'n' roll.

In addition to a deep belief in the power of culture, those on both sides of
this debate share one other characteristic as well: a deep ignorance of the history of the concept of culture and its real role in shaping behavior. Moreover,
they are ignorant of their own ignorance. Culture, after all, is something that
we all think we understand, and we all know that we are what our culture
makes us. We don't need science, do we, to explain to us its role in shaping
behavior and society? Yet, it is precisely because culture is such an important
concept in our society and, increasingly, in our political lives that we *do* need
such a science, a science of behavior that includes a clearly defined concept of
culture and that uses it along with other concepts to help us understand people's behavior not only in other societies but also in our own. Until very recently, this was not really possible. Scientific knowledge simply had not
grown to the point where it could make much use of the information we
now have about the cultures and behaviors of people around the world.
Now, at long last, science *can* study human behavior, and it needs the culture
concept to do it. The purpose of this book is to explain how such an evolutionary and cultural science of human behavior can be developed and to examine some of the benefits we might reap as this revolution in the behavioral

sciences transforms our understanding of who we are—as individuals, as members of cultural groups, and as human beings.

Mr. Tylor's Science

But as soon as we set out to use the concept of culture to study behavior, we run up against a major problem: What *is* culture, anyway? Not even anthropologists, who for many years had the concept virtually to themselves, have been able to agree on a single, clear, and logical definition of the term. Some include virtually everything associated with our species in the category. One anthropologist I know defines culture as "the sum total of all human experience." Most popular definitions are not quite so all-inclusive, but typically they do include behavior and the material things people produce in the category of culture. Other anthropologists choose to whittle it down to just its most basic bits, such as the knowledge, beliefs, values, traditions, and other sorts of information that people pass from generation to generation. Before we can get on with the task of using culture in the scientific study of behavior, we first need to settle on a good, useful definition.

Any discussion of the concept of culture must begin with Edward Burnett Tylor, the Englishman who gave the term its first technical definition. Tylor was born in 1832 to a middle-class family of English Quakers, leading some to speculate that his membership in a religious minority fostered in him an interest in cultural differences. What is clear is that his religion meant that he could not study at Oxford or Cambridge, which at the time were open only to members of the official Church of England. Instead of having a standard university education, Tylor studied at Quaker schools before joining his family's foundry business when he was only 16. When he was twenty, he was diagnosed with early symptoms of tuberculosis, and he traveled first to Cuba and then to Mexico in search of relief. He found not only relief, but also culture, and in 1861 he produced his first book, an account of his travels through Mexico.[5]

Ten years and a lot of serious research later, Tylor began his pivotal book *Primitive Culture* with this definition of culture: "that complex whole which includes knowledge, belief, art, law, morals, custom, and any other capabilities and habits acquired by man as a member of society."[6] His work on culture led to wide acclaim and, eventually, his appointment as the first professor of anthropology at any university in the world, which, ironically for Tylor, was at Oxford. So dominant was Tylor's thinking in the new discipline that when another scholar referred to it as "Mr. Tylor's science," the label stuck.[7]

The service Tylor provided was in shedding much of the baggage traditionally associated with the term "culture." For instance, after Tylor it was no
longer acceptable, at least among anthropologists, to see culture as a limited
commodity that some people have and some people don't. Culture, to anthropologists, is not shorthand for fine art, classical music, and good table
manners. It is, rather, something that everyone and every society has. Tylor's
definition also gave the new discipline of anthropology a clear, important,
and enormous subject matter, which helped it to get on its feet and stake a
claim to a broad relevance to an understanding of the human condition.

Though more than a century has passed since Tylor offered his definition
and though many liters of ink have been spilled in search of a better one, his
is still the definition dominating the discipline of anthropology. It is, for example, the definition enshrined in the majority of anthropology textbooks
and therefore taught to most anthropology students. I have surveyed twenty
introductory cultural anthropology textbooks—all that I could find published in the 1990s—and the definitions given by more than three quarters
of them are essentially the same as Tylor's. A typical modernized Tylorean definition is "Everything that people have, think, and do as members of a society." The most recent textbook in my collection simply quotes Tylor's definition verbatim.[8]

The problem with Tylor's definition is that it really isn't very helpful if our
goal is to understand why people do what they do. In short, it includes too
much. Specifically, it includes behavior—the "habits acquired by man as a
member of society." Because behavior is precisely what we are trying to explain—why do those people over there dress the way they do, eat the food
they eat, organize their families that way, and so on—including behavior in
the category of culture makes it impossible to use culture to explain anything
about behavior. The ultimate goal of any science, including a science of behavior, is to come up with what philosophers call "fundamental" explanations.[9] The only way to do this is to explain things in terms outside themselves. To the extent that we explain things in terms of themselves, we don't
really explain anything. This is akin to the idea that a good definition of a
word is one that does not use the word itself. A definition of a word in terms
of itself or an explanation of a phenomenon in terms of itself is circular and
meaningless. What this means for culture is that if we include behavior in
the category of culture then it becomes impossible to separate the two. All
behavior is "cultural behavior" because all behavior *is* culture. To explain that
people do this, that, or the other thing because of their culture is then to say
nothing that we didn't already know.

This situation, as scientifically unsatisfying as it is, appears to make a lot of people quite happy. It allows them to appear to be explaining something without really explaining anything, and, better yet, it allows them to do so while at the same time adhering to the politically popular notion that all human behavior is cultural and therefore learned and therefore malleable. However, anyone who feels this way should take note that a number of other behavioral scientists are also quite happy with Tylor's all-too-sweeping definition of culture for an entirely different reason: Because it is so useless to any real understanding of behavior, they argue that the whole concept of culture—and those who study it—can safely be ignored.

If we are to develop a real science of behavior that does take culture seriously, as we must eventually do, then how should we proceed? If there is a baby in Tylor's great big tub of a definition, how do we distinguish it from the bathwater?

Words and Deeds

> Perhaps the central methodological problem of the social sciences springs from recognition that often there is a disparity between lingual and social-motor types of behavior.
>
> —C. Wright Mills[10]

> How come you say you will when you won't
> Tell me you do, baby, when you don't
>
> —Carl Perkins, "Honey Don't"

While flying home from field research in Kenya a few years ago, the thought occurred to me that I am not entirely unlike Dolly Parton. I owe this epiphany to the movie *Straight Talk*, which had arrived quickly in airplanes after only a very brief stop in theaters. In the movie Parton plays Shirlee, a woman who is wise far beyond her few years of education and who, through a series of misunderstandings, finds herself impersonating a psychologist on a call-in radio show. A crucial turning point in the plot comes when Shirlee is confronted by the wife of a man to whom she had recently given advice—bad advice, as it turned out, thanks to a lie the man had told Shirlee. The woman asks, "You think everybody that calls you is telling you nothing but the truth?" Shirlee replies, "Well, I thought, well, sure, why, why would they lie?"

Well, why would they? Or, more broadly and more interestingly, why would people say things about themselves that do not mesh with their behavior? Why, in C. Wright Mills' somewhat antiquated sociologese, are there so often disparities "between lingual and social-motor types of behavior"? It turns out that this is just the wedge we need to pry open the culture concept, pick it apart, and turn it into something that we can use to better understand human behavior.

I was in Kenya studying a group of people called the Mukogodo, whom I had been studying since 1985. The Mukogodo are interesting for a variety of reasons. What initially attracted me to them was their unusual history: They are one of the last people on Earth to have lived in caves, having moved out of their old rockshelter homes and taken up livestock raising only about sixty to seventy years ago. Yet, the main reason I returned to study them again a few years ago was not because of their history, but rather because of how they treat their children. The Mukogodo are good and loving parents, but it turns out that, like many parents around the world, they are not completely even-handed. Specifically, they tend to take better care of their daughters than their sons. This is a very unusual pattern. It is much easier to find societies in which boys are treated better than girls. But Mukogodo parents hold their daughters more of the time than they do their sons, stay closer to them, nurse them more, and are more likely to take them for medical care. As a result, Mukogodo girls grow more quickly, compared to well-nourished American children, than Mukogodo boys, and they do not suffer as much as boys from childhood mortality.[11]

While my wife, Beth Leech, and I were studying the Mukogodo in 1986, we also noticed three very obvious cases of child neglect, and all three involved boys. One was a boy who was diagnosed by the Catholic mission's physician as suffering from malnutrition. He was thin, weak, and listless. His sister, in comparison, was healthy, lively, and well fed. Another was a toddler boy suffering from an eye infection. We suggested to his mother that she should take him for treatment, but she refused. Another boy of about six years had a large festering wound behind one ear for the entire year we were in the field. We tried bandaging it a couple of times, but it did not heal until after we left and someone from the mission happened through his area, spotted it, and gave it a really good dressing. That boy is still alive but now almost totally deaf. I do not know whether the infection had anything to do with his deafness, but the coincidence is disturbing. When we asked his parents why they did not take him to the dispensary, they argued that it was too expensive, but they did not hesitate to take either of their two daughters for treatment.

As sad as it is for little Mukogodo boys, this favoritism toward girls appears to make good sense for Mukogodo parents. Mukogodo girls have good futures ahead of them, while many Mukogodo boys do not. Virtually all Mukogodo girls can expect to marry and have families, and they often marry wealthy men from neighboring tribes. But because the Mukogodo were so recently cave-dwelling hunters and gatherers, they are despised by their neighbors and are poor even by the standards of rural Africa. As a result, many Mukogodo men have had a hard time getting married, particularly because they not only have to be able to support their future family but also to pay a substantial bridewealth—several head of cattle and sheep is typical—to their future in-laws. Many Mukogodo men, especially in the past, have either never married or have had to delay their marriages until late in life.

After hearing this story, many people assume that the Mukogodo are somehow teaching one another, either verbally or perhaps in some more subtle way, to treat daughters better than sons. But favoring daughters is precisely the opposite of what the Mukogodo say they do, and they appear to be unaware that they are even doing it. Culturally and socially, the Mukogodo are part of the world of the Maasai, a group of East African herders who have become relatively famous in the West, perhaps because they are so photogenic in their red cloaks and elaborate beads. Before European colonization, the Maasai dominated much of the East African interior. Since leaving their caves, the Mukogodo have virtually become Maasai, speaking their language, following their religion and rituals, and living like them in every way possible. In addition, they have intermarried with the Maasai at a very high rate, so that knowledge, ideas, and beliefs—particularly those, such as ideas about child care, that are likely to be carried mainly by women—have been mixed to such an extent that the Mukogodo are indistinguishable from other Maasai.

Maasai peoples, the Mukogodo included, are strongly male biased in their spoken attitudes and beliefs. In 1986 Beth interviewed more than a hundred Mukogodo women about their reproductive histories and goals. Included in each interview was a question about how many children of each sex they would like to have. This struck many of the women as a patently ridiculous. After all, it is God who decides such things, not them. But many women did express an opinion, and the thrust was clear: Mukogodo mothers have a slight stated preference for sons, not daughters. In 1993, I hired a Mukogodo woman as a field assistant to do similar interviews with a smaller sample of women, and she found an even stronger male bias in their preferences. The preference for sons makes little sense given the behavior of Mukogodo parents, but it makes a lot of sense given their self-identification as Maasai. To Maasai, maleness is associated with good characteristics, such as honor, prestige, and respect, while femaleness is associated with many bad qualities, including imperfection and cowardice. It is no wonder that Mukogodo mothers would fail to express a preference for girls over boys, but it *is* a wonder that this is how they in fact behave.[12]

It turns out that the Mukogodo are not the only people who are able to say one thing about whether they prefer boys or girls and do another to their actual children. Another group of African pastoralists, the Herero of Botswana, favor their daughters over their sons to such an extent that boys are three times more likely than girls to die in infancy and about twice as likely to die in childhood. The !Kung[13] neighbors of the Herero remark that the Herero "take their daughters to their hearts" and "refuse their sons," expressing disgust at the disgraceful way the Herero treat their sons. But the Herero themselves consistently deny that children of either sex are favored, arguing instead that witchcraft is responsible for the boys' high death rates. On a Pacific Ocean atoll called Ifaluk, the situation is reversed: parents do express a preference for one sex—in this case, girls—but they do not consistently favor girls over boys. Rather, high status Ifalukese mothers and fathers spend more time caring for their sons while only lower status parents spend more time with their daughters.[14]

South Asia is an area famous for widespread favoritism toward sons. It is well known, for example, that some Indian parents have used modern methods to determine the sex of their fetuses just so that they can abort females, and there is an ample literature documenting that many Indian and Bangladeshi girls are treated quite poorly compared to their brothers, who commonly receive more food and better medical care. In this case, there is, overall, a good correspondence between statements and actions. Indian parents not only often treat sons better than daughters, most also will say that they want more sons than daughters. However, there is an interesting sort of slippage between what South Asian parents say and what they do. When economic and marital prospects for girls are bad compared to those for boys, the culture of son preference and the treatment of sons and daughters match up quite well. But when girls' opportunities for jobs and good marriages improve, daughters suddenly are treated better. In Bangladesh, for example, garments manufactured largely by women have surpassed jute and tea as the nation's most lucrative export, and many Bangladeshi women are now earning more than their husbands. As a result, women are being seen as valuable members of a household rather than drains on resources, and men are trying to bring more working women—sisters, wives, daughters—into their households.[15]

In the United States, studies on racism have uncovered many interesting examples of discrepancies between attitudes and behavior, though the direction of the mismatch is not always what one might expect.[16] For example, back in the 1930s, when racism was more socially acceptable than now, a sample of restaurateurs and hotel owners were asked whether they would serve Chinese people. Although only two of the 256 businesses surveyed said they would serve Chinese, when actual Chinese people attempted to get service at the same businesses they were refused service at only one hotel. Happily, racist behavior seemed to be much less prevalent than racist attitudes.[17]

These days, of course, racism is not socially acceptable to many Americans, and it is probably more often the case that people who claim to be unprejudiced actually behave differently when given the chance. For example, as southern Whites were quick to point out, northerners often failed to live up to their rhetoric in favor of racial equality when issues such as neighborhood integration and school busing came to their part of the country in the 1960s and 1970s. Sociological research back in the 1950s uncovered just this sort of discrepancy between rhetoric and reality in a strongly unionized working class community. The official ideology of the union was strongly behind acceptance of African Americans at work, and, indeed, there was a very strong correlation between how involved individuals were in union activities and how much they accepted African-American co-workers. On the other hand, a local community organization, called the Civic Club, had an equally clear ideology. In the words of the Club's president, its "main purpose . . . is to keep up the bar against the colored element moving in here. That was the purpose when it was first organized and that is still the purpose today." The secretary-treasurer was equally clear: "Of course we are interested in keeping this community white. . . . We have had several intrusions but all of them have been eliminated by direct action of the club." What is interesting about this is that the very individuals who were the most accepting of African Americans at work were more often than not the least tolerant of them in the neighborhood.[18]

Also in the 1950s, sociologists documented a similar mismatch between American college students' statements about racial prejudice and their own actions. The students were first asked a series of questions about race relations. Then they were shown some slides of African-American and European-American men and women seated together talking and asked whether they would be willing to have their photographs taken with someone of the other sex and race. They were given a range of options, including refusing to be photographed, allowing the photographs to be taken but used only for limited research purposes, and allowing the photographs to be used in a national campaign advocating racial integration. For the most part, the less prejudiced students were more agreeable to the idea of being photographed than the more prejudiced ones, but a large minority of both relatively prejudiced and relatively unprejudiced students did the opposite of what would be expected from their stated attitudes.[19]

Similar sorts of discrepancies have been uncovered in many different circumstances. Again back in the 1950s, the official morality about alcohol consumption in one small Kansas town was as clear as gin: It is wrong, and only bums and lower-class people do it. But, not surprisingly, many self-described teetotalers actually did drink, including several members of the Women's Christian Temperance Union who not only drank privately but also served alcohol to guests in their homes.[20] At the other end of the American social spectrum, an insightful and sensitive ethnographic study of a group of poor African-American men in the 1960s uncovered a different sort of discrepancy between attitudes and behavior. When it came to women, the men talked a good game, but their actual behavior usually did not live up to their talk. According to their rhetoric, women exist to be used, both as sex objects and as sources of income. In short, "a man should take what he can get when he can get it." In fact, men often failed to take advantage of women who were available to them and broke off relationships with women who supported them economically. They also often developed meaningful, personal, intimate relationships with women built on mutual love and respect rather than on the ruthless ethic of righteous exploitation they were so eager to trumpet.[21]

Of course, Americans are by no means unique in their ability to say one thing and do another. A detailed study of attitudes and behavior among a group of Mexican Indians, for instance, revealed the same sort of discrepancy between attitudes and behaviors seen in the other studies. The men in Zinacantan, a Tzotzil-speaking township in the Mexican state of Chiapas, say that they have traditional values such as respect for those who work hard, those who are religious, and those who avoid the trappings of modern, Western society, including modern medicine as opposed to native healers. There is, however, no correlation between how strongly men say they hold these values and their actual behavior. In fact, those who are the most devoted to religion are a bit more likely than others to visit Western physicians.[22]

Baby Versus Bathwater

As Shirlee found out the hard way, the simplest way to explain these discrepancies would be to put it all down to lying. Although lying does indeed happen around the world, this will not get us very far. Certainly Mukogodo parents are being honest when they say they want more boys than girls, Zinacantecan men are being honest when they say they value religiosity, and the business owners back in the 1930s were being honest when they said that they would not serve Chinese people. A more plausible explanation in some of these situations is that people's rhetoric has not caught up with their reality. In South Asia, for example, it may be that the economic prospects of women have changed so rapidly that cultural norms about how sons and daughters should be treated have yet to catch up.[23] On the other hand, sometimes rhetoric runs ahead of behavior, as among the college students who knew that they weren't supposed to be racially prejudiced but who had a hard time not acting that way.

These discrepancies between attitudes and behavior help to clarify and highlight an important gap in our understanding of human actions. As Roy d'Andrade, an anthropologist at the University of California at San Diego, put it recently,

> there is no clear relation between *culture* and *action*. Of course, one can say "people do what they do because their culture makes them do it." The problem with this formulation is that it does not explain anything. Do people always do what their culture tells them to? If they do, why do they? If they don't, why don't they? And how does culture make them do it? Unless there is some specification of how culture "makes" people do what they do, no explanation has been given.[24]

Fortunately, these sorts of discrepancies between attitudes and behavior can also help us see a way out of the current mess and toward a science of behavior that makes constructive use of culture. Clearly, there is a lot of slippage among the different elements of Tylor's broad definition of "culture," and particularly between the ideational parts of it—knowledge, belief, morals, and so on—and the behavioral part of it. One way to approach the problem of redefining the term "culture," then, is to throw one of these elements out and keep the others. If behavior is what we want to explain, and if we want a culture concept that allows us to explain it in a fundamental way, then the baby we need to keep is the ideational part.

This, in fact, is something that has been underway among anthropologists for decades, although it does not seem to have had much effect on those who write the textbooks. As long ago as the 1950s, some anthropologists were inclined "strongly to exclude behavior as such from culture" because, they noted wisely, "there is also human behavior not determined by culture."[25]

The usefulness of a limited, ideational definition of culture became more widely understood in the 1950s when anthropologists began to study cognition—the process of knowing—and began to think of culture as a sort of knowledge.[26] Culture did have something to do with behavior, but it was not the same thing as behavior. Some of them used an analogy with language to make their point. Just as the rules of language tell people how to speak but are not the same thing as speech, so does culture guide people's behavior without being the same thing as behavior. As Princeton anthropologist Clifford Geertz has persuasively written, culture is patterns *for* behavior, not patterns *of* behavior.[27] Culture is neither the act of baking a cake nor the cake itself, but the recipe, the *socially transmitted information* that tells a person how to bake a cake. By separating behavior from culture we can finally hope to use the culture concept to actually explain behavior in a fundamental way—in terms outside itself—without making the mistake of thinking that all behavior is caused by culture or that behavior reflects the influence of culture in any simple or straightforward way. Discrepancies between behavior and culture are suddenly transformed from embarrassments to be swept under the great rug of Tylor's definition to exciting opportunities for insights into the real relationship between behavior and culture.

Such Stuff as Chairs Are Made Of

The idea of culture as something purely ideational, something from which we explicitly exclude material things and behavior, has traditionally not sat well with a lot of anthropologists and other behavioral and social scientists who see themselves as working in the materialistic tradition of the natural sciences. They fear that ideational definitions turn the concept into something ethereal and incorporeal, something that we have no hope of ever measuring or observing directly. Defining culture simply as "knowledge" or "information," they argue, simply "reifies" it, meaning that it treats something that is essentially unreal as if it were real. Including behavior and material objects in the category of culture is comforting because those are things that we can actually observe and measure. Many archaeologists, for example, are fond of the phrase "material culture" as a way of refering to the artifacts they recover from ancient societies. Materialists feel that the only way we will ever be able to develop a true science of culture is with a traditional, Tylorean definition of culture, one that includes material things and the behaviors that produce them.

At the same time that the materialists have shied away from ideational definitions of culture, those who have embraced them have mostly belonged to anthropology's other camp, those who see themselves as working not in the tradition of the natural sciences but rather in that of the humanities. Referring to their work by such labels as "symbolic," "structural," "interpretive," and "hermeneutic" anthropology, they see their goal not so much as to explain behavior as to interpret it in much the same way as, say, an art critic interprets the work of a sculptor. The mere fact that humanistic researchers are so enamored of ideational definitions of culture is enough to make many of us who are more inclined towards a scientific approach wary.

In recent years, however, a growing number of scientific anthropologists and others in the behavioral sciences have come to appreciate the usefulness of an ideational definition of culture. Some of the confusion over the value of the idea that we should use the term "culture" to refer only to socially transmitted information lies in a failure to understand that while culture is indeed not directly observable, it is nonetheless real. Real things that are not directly observable are routine things in many sciences, and scientists study them all the time. No one, for example, has ever observed a quark, electron, or any other subatomic particle in the same way that we can observe, say, someone cooking dinner. All we can observe are the effects of those particles, and from those effects we infer, based on theories and long strings of inferences founded on previous scientific findings, that they must exist. For that matter, no one has ever directly observed the earth's core, but it is easy to find confident statements by geologists about its makeup because they can observe its effects on other things (like magnets) and then make logical deductions about it.

Culture is the same way. We can observe it only through its effects on behavior, not directly, inferring its presence when behavior forms certain patterns and its absence when those patterns are not present. Consider again, for example, the Mukogodo and their children. There is no evidence that culture is behind the favoritism shown daughters. Favoritism toward daughters clearly is not being passed on verbally, since what comes out of Mukogodo parents' mouths is favoritism toward sons, not daughters. And it does not appear to be passed on through observations of behavior because so many of the women who display favoritism toward their daughters are recent arrivals to the Mukogodo, having been raised among neighboring peoples who show no evidence of daughter favoritism. After all that evidence, it would be folly to argue that socially transmitted information—culture—is at the root of Mukogodo parental behavior. Things are made doubly difficult for students of culture in that we must study it through behavior and its products even though not all behavior is caused by culture. This does not make studying culture impossible. And it most certainly does not mean that anything abstract is being reified by the concept of culture. But if culture is real, then of what is it made? Of course culture exists in the same material world as the rest of the things in our universe, and so it must take physical form somewhere. It does so as mental representations inside people's heads. In this sense, "material culture" does exist, not as stone tools, chairs, and pottery shards, but as combinations of neurochemicals and electrical charges in people's brains.[28]

Memes and Milk Bottles

Some of those who have begun to use an ideational definition of culture in their research on behavior could scarcely be accused of having any dangerous humanistic sympathies. Consider, for example, the growing field known variously as "cultural transmission theory," "dual inheritance theory," "evolutionary culture theory," and, most simply, "memetics." Their central idea is best summed up by the word meme, which rhymes (not coincidentally) with gene. A meme is a culture trait—a bit of socially shared information. Cultural transmission theorists, or memeticists, study the transmission and evolution of culture traits in the same way that geneticists and evolutionary biologists study the transmission and evolution of genetically based traits. A meme might be a clothing fashion, a popular song, or a religious belief. Some memes are good at spreading from mind to mind, leading some people to refer to them as "mind viruses," while others have a hard time being picked up and passed along. Some memes are especially good at being spread because they encourage their bearers to spread them. Consider, for example, proselytizing religions. One of the ways that believers in such religions can demonstrate their belief is to go out and tell others about it. The word "meme" itself is a very successful meme, having become common in popular writing as well as among scholars since it was coined more than twenty years ago by the biologist Richard Dawkins.[29] As memes spread and fade, whole cultures change, giving cultural transmission theorists plenty of raw material for their research.

And that research is nothing if not rigorous and scientific. Virtually all cultural-transmission theory is highly technical and mathematical, as far in style and spirit as one can get from the interpretive, touchy-feely approach of the humanists. Some of the mathematical models used are borrowed from epidemiology, the study of how diseases spread through populations. Others mimic the style of population biology, conceiving of cultures as populations of memes just as genes exist in populations of organisms.[30]

Another group of scientists who make good use of an ideationally defined concept of culture are those who study culture among animals. To many people, of course, the idea of "animal culture" is an oxymoron because culture has so often been defined as something uniquely human, something that distinguishes us from other species. Animals may make tools, they may be able to use a little language, they may even hunt and kill members of their own species, but we are the only species with culture, right? Other species may have "socially transmitted information," but, they argue, let's not call it "culture." And if we are the only species with culture, then certainly that justifies a fundamental separation of the study of human behavior from the study of nonhuman behavior.

But other species do indeed have socially transmitted information, and a growing number of animal behaviorists can no longer deny calling it "culture." One of the best known examples of animal culture, involving titmice, was discovered in Britain in the 1950s. Apparently an innovative bird discovered that it could get a good, fatty meal by pecking through the aluminum foil caps on milk bottles left outside in the old days of daily home milk deliveries. Other birds watched the behavior, imitated it, and it spread rapidly. Similarly, variations in bird song dialects have been shown to be transmitted from bird to bird. Japanese macaques, which are much closer relatives of humans than titmice, have been observed to learn from each other how to wash potatoes and how to separate wheat grains left on a beach from sand by tossing handfuls in the water and scooping up the floating grains. And, closest of all to humans, chimpanzees have been shown to transmit information about termite-fishing, nut-cracking, and other ways of getting food. Although examples like these are interesting, their novelty and obscurity help to highlight that the vast majority of animal behavior has nothing to do with culture. Precisely because so much of animal behavior does not involve culture, animal behaviorists have been able to see much more clearly than those of us who study human behavior that the concept of culture cannot both include behavior and be truly useful in explaining behavior.[31]

Among humans, on the other hand, culture is so pervasive that we have a hard time even conceiving of behavior that is not primarily a product of culture. As a result, all of the different ways of life shown by people in our society and around the world are seen as products of culture, and, increasingly, not just culture *per se* but cultural diversity in particular has become a political as well as a scientific issue. But the politicization of cultural diversity begs one central question: How diverse are human societies, anyway? To answer that, it might be useful to let our imaginations run free for a while and consider the possibility of diversity even greater than what we find here on Earth, no matter what species we examine.

2

Natural Kinds

. . . the contemplation in natural science of a wider domain than the actual leads to a far better understanding of the actual.

—A. S. Eddington[1]

No practical biologist interested in sexual reproduction would be led to work out the detailed consequences experienced by organisms having three or more sexes: yet what else should he do if he wishes to understand why the sexes are, in fact, always two?

—R. A. Fisher [2]

The Gethenians

In the late 1960s, thanks to the work of ethnographer O. T. Oppong, a fascinating new people living in a little-explored place called Gethen were brought to light. Because Gethen is nearly inaccessible today and inhospitably cold, some researchers think it likely that the Gethenians' ancestors migrated there during a warm interglacial period tens of thousands of years ago. During their many millennia of isolation, the Gethenians developed a unique culture that has been the object of much study and speculation.

Gethenian social life is especially remarkable for the wide and unusual range of options it allows concerning sexual ties and familial organization. Sexual relations, called *kemmer*, are usually enjoyed in pairs, but promiscuous mating in communal homes, called kemmerhouses, is also very common and fully accepted. A third option is to "vow kemmering." Although this is essentially like monogamous marriage, vow kemmering does not have any legal status in Gethen.

Gethen is also notable for its extreme sexual egalitarianism. Unlike so many of the societies with which anthropologists are familiar, Gethen is not at all dominated by males. Gethenians call the mother "the parent of the flesh," and they place great stress on the tie between mothers and offspring. Their rule of descent is, accordingly, strictly matrilineal. Gethenians also do not have any sexual division of labor, apart from the fact that female Gethenians nurse their children for the first six to eight months. The idea that a person's gender would determine his or her role or status in society is unknown in Gethen. Some might find it tempting to argue that the lack of male control over Gethenian affairs explains the absence of warfare in Gethen, but it would be wrong to say that Gethenians are truly peaceful. Oppong reports that even though organized aggression is unknown, Gethenians are still quite competitive and even capable of violence: "They kill each other readily by ones and twos; seldom by tens and twenties; never by hundreds or thousands."

So far, Gethen may sound rather exotic, but not beyond the realm of ethnographic possibility. If not for the lousy weather, it might even make for an interesting visit. But the only place that you will find O. T. Oppong and the Gethenians is between the covers of Ursula K. Le Guin's *The Left Hand of Darkness*.[3] Le Guin's novel is a work of social science fiction, a sort of extraterrestrial ethnography that explores the relationships among sexuality, psyche, and society. Throughout the book, Le Guin demonstrates her trademark sociological inventiveness and cultural sensitivity, which anthropologists such as myself often like to think are attributable to her parentage. Her father, Alfred Kroeber, was a pioneer in American anthropology and founded the anthropology program at the University of California, while her mother, Theodora Kroeber, was the author of *Ishi in Two Worlds*,[4] a biography of a California Indian. While the Kroebers concentrated on societies that actually have existed, Le Guin has chosen instead to imagine new ones.

Just as a biologist interested in the problem of why there are two sexes might do well to imagine a species with three or more, anthropologists interested in cultural variations among human societies might do well to imagine, as Le Guin has done, societies with cultural traits other than those we find in the real world. By imagining such nonexistent societies as Gethen, we may be better able to understand not only the great power of culture to influence behavior and create variability among human societies but also its limitations.

Imagining Diversity

Not all imaginary societies and cultural practices are to be found in science fiction. Some are even enshrined in scholarly books and are the foundation blocks of whole academic disciplines. Consider, for example, the notion that while adolescence in Western societies is a time of emotional upheaval and conflict within the family over a girl's new sexuality, adolescence for people on the Pacific islands of Samoa is a trouble-free time, marked by sexual experimentation and exploration. This was the picture painted by Margaret Mead in her 1928 book *Coming of Age in Samoa*,[5] published when Mead was only 26. Mead had left for Samoa three years earlier after receiving her training and marching orders from the founder of academic anthropology in the United States, Franz Boas. At that time, as now, culture was also a hot, political topic as a counterpoint to racist and eugenicist thought popular at the time. Then, as now, immigrants were on the receiving end of much of the racist rhetoric, and even very mainstream politicians got into the act, using the new science of genetics as a cloak for anti-immigrant sentiments. Calvin Coolidge, for example, said that "biological laws tell us that certain divergent people will not mix or blend. The Nordics propagate themselves successfully. With other races, the outcome shows deterioration on both sides."[6] Boas, himself an immigrant, had worked hard to combat such notions, offering instead the idea of cultural—rather than genetic—determinism. We are not what our genes make us, but rather what our cultures make us, he argued.

Mead's mission at the young age of 23 was to provide evidence for the extreme cultural determinist position, and that she did, claiming not only that Samoan adolescence differed from that of Americans, but also that Samoans in general do not feel strong emotions or form deep, long-lasting personal relationships with one another. According to Mead, the Samoan study showed that how one experiences adolescence, and, by extension, most of the rest of the human experience, is culturally determined and highly flexible. Her findings were so striking and her book so readable that they quickly became part not only of American popular culture but also part of the foundation of the discipline of anthropology and its insistence ever since on the overriding importance of culture in human affairs.

The only problem with Mead's picture of Samoan adolescence was that it was not much more real than Gethen. In 1987, more than six decades after Mead left Samoa, an old Samoan woman named Fa'apua'a Fa'amū came forward to let the world know what had really happened back in 1926 when Mead had interviewed her and her friends. She reported in a sworn deposition that, as a prank, they had told Mead the exact opposite of the truth about Samoan sexual behavior and values. In Fa'apua'a's own words, "Fofoa and I would pinch one another and say: 'We spend the nights with boys, yes, with boys!' She must have taken it seriously but I was only joking. As you know Samoan girls are terrific liars when it comes to joking. But Margaret accepted our trumped-up stories as though they were true. . . . We just fibbed and fibbed to her."[7]

Samoa was just one of several places where Mead did fieldwork, and, as is common in anthropology as young anthropologists return to societies that have already been studied, some of her other findings have also been questioned. For example, in 1935 Mead published the influential book *Sex and Temperament in Three Primitive Societies*,[8] which was designed to demonstrate the great flexibility possible in male and female roles and personalities across societies. One of the societies included in the book was the Tchambuli (or Chambri) of Papua New Guinea. Among the Tchambuli, Mead wrote, the positions of the sexes are reversed compared to what we find in most societies. For instance, she argued, Tchambuli women are more economically productive than the men, doing most of the fishing and trading with neighboring groups, while Tchambuli men are dependents who spend much of their time painting, dancing, preening, and gossiping. The implication, of course, is that male and female roles, personalities, and temperaments are as flexible and as much shaped by culture as, say, how people experience adolescence.

When the Tchambuli were studied later by other anthropologists, though, their distinctiveness largely vanished. Yes, Tchambuli women produce more of the food than the men, but this is true in a great many male-dominated societies. The Tchambuli appear to fit a common pattern in which the women produce most of the calories but the distribution of the fruits of their labors is largely up to the men. Mead's Tchambuli, it seems, like Mead's Samoa and Le Guin's Gethen, never really existed.[9]

Timeless Misconceptions

Several other less well known but equally fascinating false examples of cultural diversity also exist in the anthropological literature about the world's people. For example, until recently many anthropologists believed that the Hopi people of Arizona have no concept of time, or, rather, that their concept of time is quite different from our own. The basic idea was that, because the Hopi language does not talk about time in the Western fashion as a flowing continuum, they do not perceive time that way.[10] This has long been used by cultural determinists to bolster their claims of extreme cultural diversity and of the power of culture, and specifically language, to shape a person's worldview. If our language does not give something a name, so goes the story, then we do not see it. Thanks to some recent and exhaustive linguistic research, we now know that the Hopi not only have a concept of time, but they can discuss it with as much complexity and subtlety as anyone else. They do talk about time as a flowing continuum, they do understand temporal units like days, weeks, months, and so on, and they do have a tense system. Far from oblivious to time, the Hopi actually seem rather obsessed with it.[11]

This notion that various people around the world do not have the "Western" concept of time is one that seems to crop up in the oddest places and for no apparent reason other than to exoticize non-Western peoples. The Maasai, for example, are sometimes said to lack a concept of the future. A character in the film version of Karen Blixen's *Out of Africa* claims that one cannot jail a Maasai because he will die because of his inability to imagine a future outside his cell. I cannot imagine anything more ridiculous about the Maasai, whose language I speak. The Maasai word for future is *kenya* (not related to the name of the country, which is pronounced slightly differently), and they also have words for later today, tomorrow, the day after tomorrow, next month, and so on. Like the Hopi, on closer examination Maasai-speakers seem not only aware of time, but are obsessed with it, routinely using a complex system of demonstrative adjectives to refer to subtle variations in the placement of objects in time, such as "that thing of long ago," "that thing of yesterday," "that thing of earlier today," "that thing of just a moment ago," and so on. No Maasai-speaker I have ever met has ever had any trouble imagining or talking about the past, present, or future.

Another old saw in the cultural determinist literature is the idea that facial expressions are learned and therefore culturally variable, that what means one thing to you and yours—a smile, say—might mean something totally different to people in New Guinea. Certainly some facial expressions *are* learned. Sticking one's tongue out means different things in different places. In America it's an insult. To the Mukogodo, it's just a polite way of pointing at things rather than pointing with a finger. But what about more basic expressions like smiling and frowning? Some researchers have argued, and no doubt many people still believe, that these things are just as learned as hairstyles or languages. But, again, recent research has shown that many basic facial expressions are common to all the world's peoples. You can take photographs of Americans making a variety of faces—frowning, smiling, or feigning surprise, contempt, or anger—and people in different societies can recognize them and their meanings very easily. This works even in societies that are so isolated that the people have little if any experience with visual images such as photographs, films, or television shows, and so have had no opportunity to learn the way the rest of the world expresses emotions. The Dani of the western part of the island of New Guinea, for example, who until recently still used only stone tools, are able to identify the emotions of people in photographs as accurately as Americans. And, conversely, when Americans are shown photographs of people from New Guinea with a variety of facial expressions, they also easily determine their meanings.[12]

Gethen, the Samoa of Mead's informants' imagination, a timeless Hopi pueblo, and a land where people smile when we would frown are just a few imaginable societies that have never existed. It is easy to think of many other combinations of social characteristics and cultural practices that may seem plausible, but that we Earthlings have never truly invented. Although humanity's diversity has long been the *raison d'être* of my own discipline, cultural anthropology, human cultures do indeed display a remarkable degree of uniformity. The tendency of cultures to stick to certain basic patterns suggests that they are not endlessly variable, bounded only by our imaginations. Rather, this tendency suggests that there are constraints acting on culture, channeling societies in certain directions and steering them away from others, and it suggests that *some thing* or *things* other than culture have profound influences on human behavior. In short, the uniformity of cultures has the potential to tell us as much about what it is to be human as can our societies' much-advertised diversity.

Ethnographic Hyperspace

Although diversity is often stated as if it were an absolute quality of human societies, it is, of course, actually a relative term and means nothing in isolation. To understand this, imagine for a moment that the world's cultures were not as diverse as they are, but instead only as diverse as, say, the cultures represented within the United States. How would we know? This is akin to the old question that asks, what if everything in the universe suddenly and simultaneously grew a thousand times larger? Of course we would never know that it had happened, because size is relative. So is cultural diversity. If the world's cultures were only half as diverse as they actually are, it is a safe bet that we cultural anthropologists would still be making our living by emphasizing that diversity and downplaying what we all have in common. The world's cultures may be diverse, but diverse compared to what?

One way to approach this question is to look at information about many different cultures. Such cross-cultural databases are often used to test ideas about societies and to look for patterns that occur across many cultures. For example, an anthropologist might ask if one type of family arrangement is more common among hunting people than among fishers, or if certain political systems are usually found in societies with castes. Answering these questions is made easier by the existence of well-organized databases, such as the Human Relations Area Files,[13] that contain systematic codes for a large variety of cultural traits. Although the emphasis in cross-cultural research is, naturally, on societies that actually exist, this approach can also throw light on those that do not, such as Gethen.

One subset of societies from the Human Relations Area Files, the *Ethnographic Atlas*,[14] contains information on more than eight hundred different cultures, coded into more than forty different variables describing each society's economy, social system, political practices, religious beliefs, and even what games they play. Each variable has different possible values, ranging from a handful to a hundred or more for complicated topics like marriage rules. To return for a moment to the world of science fiction, you can think of it as an ethnographic hyperspace—an imaginary space with many more than the usual three spatial and one temporal dimension of our own space— with each society occupying a single point whose location is described by the values of its variables. The vast majority of points in this space are not occupied by any known society, and probably never have been or ever will be. The rarity of occupied sites in the ethnographic hyperspace is easy to see by calculating the total number of possible combinations of the variables. If all of the variables in the *Ethnographic Atlas* are included, the number of imaginable types of societies is this number: 120,000,000,000,000,000,000, 000,000,000,000,000,000,000,000,000,000.

This is a 12 followed by fifty-two zeros. I don't know what to call this number, but it is safe to say that it is large.

Even such an astronomical estimate may not do justice to the room that exists, in principle, for cultural diversity greater than we actually see. After all, a table of variables such as the *Ethnographic Atlas* is, by definition, a bad place to look for uniformity. If all peoples do something exactly the same way, it would be senseless to provide a variable for it, just on the slim chance that a place such as Gethen might be discovered. However, anthropologists occasionally have imagined practices that seem like logical possibilities, but that have never been observed. By their very nonexistence such customs may suggest something about the constraints underlying cultural uniformity. For example, it is common in matrilineal societies for newly married couples to live with the husband's mother's brother (i.e., avunculocality). Because with matrilineality, property and positions of status are mostly inherited from a man to his sister's sons, such a residence pattern makes sense because it puts a man where he needs to be: with his mother's brother and other matrilineal kin. However, the opposite pattern, called amitalocality, in which the newly-weds live with the wife's father's sister's family, so far is known to exist only in ethnographic hyperspace, perhaps somewhere not far from Gethen.[15]

Human Universals

Human societies share a great many more features than just the absence of an obscure curiosity like amitalocality. How many universals there are in human societies is something that neither I nor many other anthropologists really appreciated until recently. My eyes were opened to universals by the work of Donald Brown, a cultural anthropologist at the University of California at Santa Barbara.[16] For most of his career, Brown was a mainstream cultural anthropologist, meaning that he placed the emphasis in his teaching and writing on cultural diversity rather than cultural uniformity. For example, he routinely used a story from his own fieldwork experience to make a point to his students about cultural diversity. While working in Brunei, a small country on the island of Borneo, he sat down on a bench with two young men, and a third man was seated at the same level on a rung of a nearby ladder. Then Brown grew tired of sitting on the bench and decided to sit on the walkway instead. Very quickly, the three young men followed suit. In Brunei, he learned, it is not polite to sit higher than another person unless you outrank him. When he implored them to go ahead and sit on the bench, they argued that it would not look right.

Viewed in one way, this is a good example of cultural diversity. Among the Mukogodo, for instance, one way to show deference to a respected guest is to give him a stool or, better yet, a hide on which to sit. That may put him at a lower level than others, but the fact that he has something to sit on shows his higher status. On the other hand, as time went on Brown was struck by the ways in which that story demonstrated some common human characteristics. For instance, the men, like people around the world, were concerned about what others might think of them, about politeness, and about rank. Even the use of highness and lowness to signify rank, while not universal, is extremely common across cultures.

Armed with this sort of insight, Brown went on to comb the literature on human societies for evidence of universals. This is a tricky business, to be sure. Searching for universals in the cross-cultural literature is a little like searching a bibliographic database: Changing the specificity of your search parameters can increase or decrease your number of "hits" dramatically. For example, a search through the ethnographic literature for any specific detail of religion—a belief in multiple gods or in spirit possession, for instance— would give one the impression of great diversity (a valid one, I might add, as long as the relativity of the concept of "diversity" is remembered), while a much broader search for the presence of religious ideas would reveal a universal pattern. According to Brown, all recorded human societies "have religious or supernatural beliefs in that they believe in something beyond the visible and palpable" . . . they "also practice magic, and their magic is designed to do such things as sustain and increase life and to win the attention of the opposite sex" . . . they "have rituals, and these include rites of passage that demarcate the transfer of an individual from one status to another."

Brown summarized his findings on universals in a book chapter titled "The Universal People,"[17] which describes an imaginary ethnic group that has all of the characteristics he has identified as universal among human societies. My expectation before reading the book—and, I imagine, that of most cultural anthropologists even now—would be that such a chapter would be quite brief given the self-evident diversity of human cultures. But Brown's "Universal People" take up ten pages of dense type, with universals appearing in everything from the details of language and grammar to social arrangements to the ubiquity of music, dance, and play. The list includes some surprises. Every society has gossip, all societies understand the idea of a lie, they all have special types of speech for special occasions, they all use narrative, and they all have poetry with lines that take about three seconds to say. Men are everywhere on average more aggressive and more likely to kill than women, though individual men and women do differ significantly from the average. Everyone has taboos on certain statements and certain foods. All societies are at least aware of dancing (though it is prohibited in some of them) and have some sort of music. Remarkably, everyone has children's music. If, as cultural determinist dogma would have it, culture is all-diverse and all-powerful, why are there any such universals? Why aren't human cultures more diverse than they apparently are?

The Great Attractor

To stretch the analogy between ethnology and cosmology a bit further, the problem we confront is a bit like that facing astronomers who want to know the locations and dimensions of dark matter in the universe. By definition, such matter does not reveal itself through the emission of radiation. Black holes, for example, have such tremendous gravity that they let no light, matter, or other radiation escape. The presence of such objects can only be inferred by their effects on other, observable objects like stars and galaxies. The most dramatic example of the effects of such dark matter is the so-called Great Attractor, a mysterious object with the mass of tens of thousands of galaxies toward which the Milky Way and its neighboring galaxies are gravitating at speeds of up to seven hundred miles per second.[18]

In short, we are in search of the Great Attractor of human culture, the unseen mass that pulls human cultures toward it and so limits their diversity. To find it, we have to look closely at the forces that shape cultural and social patterns and ask which of them are sources of uniformity rather than diversity. There are several possibilities. The least flattering one is that although a variety of better, more beneficial and rewarding sociocultural arrangements are possible, we Earthling humanoids are just not intelligent enough to imagine other possible social arrangements.

Another possibility is that my estimate of 12 plus all the zeros overstates the number of societies that are really plausible. This would be true if many of the variables in the cross-cultural data files were highly correlated. If societies' inheritance practices always matched up with their marriage patterns, for example, then these should really be considered as just one variable, not two. Many such correlations among different variables are known. One study[19] of the cross-cultural data found that there were enough regularities in the relationships among some aspects of culture that just nine different variables were needed to describe a sample of more than five hundred societies from around the world. Only one variable was necessary to describe the variations in sociopolitical stratification from egalitarian societies to those with rigid caste systems. Subsistence practices ranging from hunting and gathering to farming and herding and family organization, including such things as variations in permitted numbers of spouses for men and women and whether descent is reckoned through men, women, or both, each required just four variables. If we recalculate the total number of possible combinations using only these variables, there are still over one hundred million possible combinations. Although this is a lot less than the number of possibilities given earlier in this chapter, it still suggests that only a tiny fraction of the points in ethnographic hyperspace are occupied.

Maybe the problem is that only certain pathways through ethnographic hyperspace are actually possible. Once a society is started on a path, it may not be able to leave it easily, and changing directions or jumping to nonadjacent points may be difficult. A society's current form is obviously a product of the way it used to be, and it may be that history itself constrains culture. This is analogous to an idea in evolutionary biology called phylogenetic inertia, which states that the power of natural selection to change a species is limited by the range of variations that could plausibly appear in the species. In other words, just because we can imagine that a particular new trait would be helpful to an organism does not mean that it will ever appear. Baboons, for instance, might find wings extremely useful for flying away from leopards or for scouting out new food sources, but there is virtually no chance that they will sprout them. The necessary modifications in baboon physiology are simply too great for such a thing to occur. Or, for a more realistic example, consider the way a man's testes are connected to his penis. The most economical way to do this necessary job would be to have a short tube that goes as directly as possible from testes to penis. But in fact our vas deferens are uneconomically long and awkwardly draped over the ureters that connect our kidneys to our bladders. This makes little sense unless we realize that the testes must have started out inside the body, which is where many other mammals have them, and migrated down to the scrotum thanks to the power of natural selection. It may have been better, in retrospect, for the plumbing involved to have been completely reworked, but evolution is incapable of that. It can only work on the variation that already exists, modifying it little by little. This is similar to the effect of wandering around one's yard with a garden hose without paying attention to the way it wraps around trees in the process.[20]

Ethnographers have often noticed a similar sort of limitation on cultural evolution, in which a society fails to alter its current habits or to adopt new ones despite advantages that may seem obvious to an outsider. This sort of cultural inertia seems to be at work among the Kipsigis of western Kenya, a group of farmers and herders who place a lot of value on having many children and grandchildren. The Kipsigis are quite frank about their desires for more children and grandchildren, and so it is no wonder that, in general, they do whatever it takes to reproduce. But there are limits to what they will do to have more children. For example, thanks to the health and nutritional benefits women get from large farms, in theory the Kipsigis would be able to have more grandchildren if they let daughters as well as sons inherit land. But the idea of letting their daughters inherit land seems never to have occurred to the Kipsigis, who are strictly patrilineal. The failure of the Kipsigis to let daughters inherit land may simply be a holdover from a time when

conditions were different. Until a few decades ago, the Kipsigis were pastoralists, and only males inherited livestock. After they took up farming, set-
tled down, and developed a system of property rights in land, they retained
their sons-only inheritance practice. Just as winged baboons are unlikely to
appear any time soon, so it seems the Kipsigis are not likely to let daughters
inherit land, no matter how beneficial it might be.[21]

Yet the Kipsigis example suggests why this idea is insufficient to explain
cultural uniformity. Although their inheritance practices seem slow to adjust,
the Kipsigis have actually been going through a period of extreme and rapid
change ever since the British took over Kenya late in the last century, shifting
from their traditional subsistence nomadic herding to sedentary farming. Recent anecdotal reports also suggest that the Kipsigis have begun to pass land
on to their sons-in-law, thus maintaining a patrilineal facade while actually
providing their daughters with much-needed land.[22]

Another Kenyan people, the Mukogodo of my own research, provide an
even more striking example of how rapidly and drastically it is possible for
cultures to change. Before 1925, the Mukogodo were a group of cave-
dwelling hunters and gatherers, subsisting on wild animals, plants, and
honey and speaking a now-forgotten language called Yaaku. As in many societies around the world, men were and are allowed to have more than one
wife, but they must pay bridewealth to their in-laws for the privilege. When
the Mukogodo lived in caves, the traditional bridewealth payment was a few
hollowed logs to be used as beehives. Thanks to a series of changes brought
on by the British, who made Kenya a colony, early in this century the Mukogodo came into increasing contact with several groups of Maasai-speaking
pastoralists, including the Samburu, Mumonyot, Ilng'wesi, and Digirri. The
last three of these groups had, like the Mukogodo, spent some time as
hunters and gatherers, but by this century they were making their living
from herds of cattle, goats, and sheep. The Mukogodo began to marry their
neighbors, and the bridewealth payments they received from their new in-
laws were in the form of livestock, rather than in the traditional Mukogodo
form of beehives. The livestock were worth a great deal more than the beehives, and many Mukogodo men married their daughters off to the pastoralists. Soon it became virtually impossible for anyone, even a Mukogodo man,
to obtain a wife for anything less than a few head of cattle, and so Mukogodo
men were forced to make a choice between becoming pastoralists themselves
or lifelong bachelorhood. As you might imagine, the choice was easy and the
change was swift. Within a few years they had abandoned their caves, built
Maasai-style houses, obtained livestock, and mostly abandoned hunting and

gathering. Even their old Yaaku language was dropped in favor of Maasai. In about a decade, they completely changed their culture, leaping from one point in ethnographic hyperspace to another.[23] Many other groups have gone through changes just as dramatic, jumping in some cases from the Stone Age to the Silicon Age in little more than a generation. These sorts of rapid behavioral changes are precisely why culture is so useful. While baboons will never sprout wings, we, as cultural animals, already have.

Gethenian Nature Versus Human Nature

Let's take another look at the Gethenians. Why is it that they have an approach to reproduction and family life differing so sharply from that of any real society? The key is that Gethenian sexual physiology is quite different from our own, and thus Gethenian nature is different from human nature. Unlike humans, Gethenians are not permanently male or female. Rather, the usual condition of a Gethenian is to be ambisexual (i.e., capable of becoming either a male or a female), similar to an ambidextrous person using either his right or his left hand. The potential for becoming one sex or the other becomes a reality for Gethenians during part of their monthly sexual cycle. Unlike humans, Gethenians are not continuously sexually receptive during the whole cycle. During the first twenty-one days of the cycle, Gethenians are sexually latent: They are neither interested in sex nor physiologically capable of it. On the twenty-second day an estrus-like period called *kemmer* begins. During the few days that *kemmer* lasts, a Gethenian individual has a very strong sex drive. When a partner in *kemmer* is found, more hormones are secreted until one becomes functionally male and the other functionally female. If the temporarily female partner does not conceive, then after *kemmer* both partners will return to the sexually latent *somer* stage for another three weeks. If she does conceive, she will remain physiologically female for about eight and a half months of gestation and six to eight months of lactation, after which she, too, will return to *somer*. Gethenians have no innate tendency to become either male or female, and they have no control over which sex they end up with during *kemmer*. Those who have given birth do not develop any female habits, and an individual who is the mother of some children might be the father of others. As no one has a permanent gender and since everybody on Gethen is potentially a childbearer, there is no sexual division of labor or domination of society by one sex.

Gethenian culture and society are constrained and directed, in large part, by Gethenian nature. Human cultures are constrained in different but no less profound ways by human nature. Thanks to the fact that all humans share a long evolutionary history together, we all inevitably have some of the same basic tendencies. Because the one imperative of natural selection is to reproduce, we ought to expect that the most fundamental commonalities among different peoples will be found in those institutions and practices that relate most closely to procreation. Those parts of the human endeavor that do not have much direct influence on reproduction—perhaps including art, music, and many aspects of religion—ought to display the greatest diversity. Although the sexual behavior of unfamiliar peoples, whether South Sea is-landers or your new neighbors with the hot tub, may seem exotic, in fact human reproductive practices are fairly uniform.

Family Resemblances

The institution of the family, in particular, is notable for its importance in re-production and for its universality. By "family" I do not mean anything so specific as the modern Western nuclear family enshrined in so many situation comedies and conservative political ideologies. I simply mean a social unit with a mother and child at its core and in which a male, often though not al-ways the biological father of the child, usually has an important role that lasts for considerably longer than the time it takes just to have sex. This may not sound like much of a definition, leaving open questions about numbers of spouses, ties to other families, and the exclusivity of the sexual relationship involved. However, it is indeed a distinctive social arrangement dominating human societies but not, for example, many other primate or, more broadly, mammal societies. Why should we have this particular behavior in common with each other but not with our closest nonhuman relatives? Is it culture, or is something else involved, such as our evolved human nature?

We can see how profoundly these family-building tendencies are rooted in our human nature by looking at instances where people have tried to pull up these roots, to create societies without families. The most famous such exper-iment is the kibbutzim of Israel. The kibbutz was to be a socialist commune, abolishing all private property, inheritance, the sexual division of labor, and sexual inequality. But the kibbutzim went beyond most other socialist exper-iments in also trying to do away with the privacy and primacy of the family. Marriage had no official sanction, and children were to be reared commu-nally in age-segregated "children's houses" rather than by their own parents.

Among the world's utopian socialist experiments, the kibbutzim are one of the rare success stories, but only because they have been willing to make some important concessions to human nature to keep the experiment alive. Although kibbutzim still give marriage little official recognition, in practice the institution of the family has become as much a part of life in kibbutzim as in any other society. Nowadays, the majority of kibbutz adults get married, and kibbutzim even finance and organize wedding parties. Although meals are eaten in common dining halls, families tend to sit together at separate tables. The attempt to house all children of kibbutz members together and to raise them collectively has also not fared well. Although parents had always visited their children daily, they quickly wanted to see more of each other. Mothers were particularly dissatisfied with the arrangement, and they began spending more and more time in the children's houses. This limited the mothers' mobility and hence their economic usefulness to the community, and it also annoyed those people, called *metaplots*, who were supposed to be supervising the children. Furthermore, almost all *metaplots* were women, and to avoid the problem of favoritism no mother was allowed to supervise her own child's group, making the system even more awkward. In many kibbutzim today, nuclear families have been reconstituted, and children's houses are little more than day care centers.[24]

The utopian religious colony in nineteenth century Oneida, New York, provided another demonstration of how difficult it can be to eliminate the human family. Oneida was the creation of John Humphrey Noyes, who preached that Christians must emulate the communism of the primitive Christian church. Noyes' communism, however, included collective ownership of property and other economic arrangements, but dealt with all sexual, familial, and emotional relationships as well. Noyes and the Oneidans saw monogamous marriage as a form of slavery, and they replaced it with a kind of group or "complex" marriage, in which all were married to all, and in which no one was supposed to develop an exclusive relationship with or feeling for anyone else. Like the kibbutzim, the Oneidans also communalized child care, housing, and educating all of their children in one building. Children were considered to be the charges of the entire community, and parents were discouraged from developing special emotional attachments to their own children. The Oneidans did not, however, trust the success of their project to the religious devotion of the community's members. To make sure that couples did not form, they kept a detailed record of every sexual encounter and even stipulated the length of time that couples could spend in bed together. This sort of routine scrutiny over sexuality enabled the Oneidans to institute what may be their most remarkable innovation: a systematic, genetic-engineering plan for their entire population called "stirpiculture." The goal of stirpiculture was to produce a race of people genetically predisposed to the achievement of spiritual perfection. When stirpiculture began, Oneidan women of childbearing age, along with some of the community's young men, signed resolutions renouncing their rights to self-ownership. They gave up the right to choose their own mates and instead proclaimed themselves to belong first to God and second to John Humphrey Noyes. Noyes, along with a small committee, then selected breeding partners for the community's members.

The bold Oneidan experiment, unlike that of the kibbutzim, did not last. After only a few years, severe strains began to show. Couples fell in love and yearned for lasting, exclusive bonds. Parents loved their own children more than those of others. And, finally, the colony was divided by an unusual political issue: Who was to have the right to initiate female virgins into the sexual life of the community? Until Noyes himself became elderly, he had always taken this task on himself. Factions developed around this issue, and eventually the community dissolved and reverted to the traditional human pattern of marriage and sexuality, without genetic bookkeeping.[25]

Although it usually seems to take an act of deliberate planning to push the family out of human society, one unplanned experiment in society without family is also known to have been performed by the Nayars of southwestern India. Before the British imposed colonial rule on their area in 1792, the Nayars were a warrior caste serving local kings and chiefs. Men were often on the move, frequently remaining away from their home villages for several months to a year. This mobility made it difficult for them to maintain exclusive sexual relations with any one woman, and true marriage did not exist. Although all Nayar girls went through a wedding-like ceremony, called the tali-rite, before puberty, it entailed none of the legal ties of marriage. Rather, completing the tali-rite allowed a girl to begin to select lovers. A woman could have many lovers, and a man might be the lover of many women. An advantage for the men was that they could visit lovers in distant places during their military excursions. Everyone remained a member of his or her household of birth. Men were expected to provide for their sisters' children, not those of their lovers.

When the reasons for the unusual Nayar system vanished, so did the system itself. British pacification of the area meant that Nayar men no longer had to spend so much time traveling, and it became possible to establish and maintain long-term, sexually-exclusive relationships with individual women. In the last two centuries, the tali-rite has been lost and lover relationships are no longer standard. The pan-human standards of marriage and the family have reasserted themselves and are now the norm.[26]

Behavioral Diversity Without Cultural Diversity

By emphasizing human universals in this chapter I run the risk of creating the false impression that universals are the products of biology while diversity is the product of culture. Indeed, this position is quite standard among cultural anthropologists, many of whom would agree that, as one anthropologist recently put it, "the essence of humanity is revealed as cultural diversity."[27] Biology may be fine for things we all have in common, but as soon as people start to behave differently from one another, it's time to get back to the concept of culture.

Unfortunately, things are not really that simple. Certainly *some* universals are the product of our shared biological heritage, and *some* behavioral diversity is clearly caused by the ways that cultural ideas have been transmitted among people over time. But the opposite is true, too: Some universals are the product of culture, and some behavioral diversity is the product of that evolved biological heritage we all have in common—human nature. The modern near-universality of cola-drinking, for example, is undoubtedly a result of cultural forces (as well as significant economic and political ones: During World War II Coca-Cola bottling plants sprung up wherever American GIs were stationed) combined with common features of our taste buds: Most people have an unlearned taste for sweet liquids. Behavioral diversity, on the other hand, can be the result solely of variable expression of our evolved propensities with no input from transmitted cultural ideas. Imagine, for example, an extraterrestrial intelligence that—in its malevolent way—replaced all the people on earth with identical jukeboxes loaded with thousands of different songs. Each jukebox is also equipped with a clock, a global positioning system, and a circuit that selects a song according to the jukebox's location, the local time, and the date. What the extraterrestrials then observe would be many of the same within-group behavioral similarities and between-group behavioral differences that are routinely cited as evidence of the power of culture: Every jukebox in Kinshasa would be playing the same song, but it would be a different one from the song playing in every jukebox in Irkutsk. But, clearly, no culture—in the limited sense of socially-transmitted information—would be involved in generating this diversity. Involved instead would be entities that, like humans, share a universal underlying design that responds to local conditions. The fact that people in Kinshasa have a lot of behavior in common with one another that is different from a lot of the common behavior of the people in Irkutsk does not by itself constitute evidence of the power of culture or the irrelevance of our shared human nature.[28]

Contrary to the expectations of most social scientists, it is quite possible to find examples among humans of behavioral diversity without any input from culture. For an example, let's return to the Mukogodo of Kenya. The favoritism they show their daughters, as described in Chapter One, makes sense given their particular situation: Little girls have good prospects, including a good possibility of marriage to men from higher-status neighboring groups, while Mukogodo men on the other hand often have trouble accumulating enough livestock to obtain a wife until late in life, if ever. Yet, maybe this is just what their culture tells them to do, and so this bit of behavioral diversity may indeed be attributable to culture. If so, we would be back to the standard line in the social sciences that universals might have something to do with biology, but diversity is all culture's doing.

However, as we have seen, favoring daughters over sons is precisely what the culture of the Mukogodo does *not* tell them to do, and they appear to be unaware that they are even doing it. In terms of their cultural beliefs about child rearing, the Mukogodo appear to be pretty much like other Maasai-speakers, with a stated preference for boys. This is not surprising, given that many Mukogodo women were born and raised among other groups, and many of those who were born as Mukogodo had mothers, grandmothers, and other relatives from other groups. Indeed, because the rearing of small children is almost entirely a women's activity, notions about child rearing are likely to be more similar across these societies than any other aspect of culture. Yet, despite this cultural similarity, there is behavioral diversity: Mukogodo parents favor their daughters, but non-Mukogodo parents do not. This last point deserves repetition and elaboration: While the Mukogodo seem to treat their daughters better than their sons, their neighbors seem to treat them about the same, perhaps even showing some favoritism toward sons. It might be tempting to argue, for example, that the Mukogodo think that girls are somehow fragile and need more care while non-Mukogodo parents don't believe this, but it is hard to see how such a difference in beliefs about child rearing could be maintained when women and the ideas they learned as girls about child rearing have been crossing the boundaries between these groups so often and for so long.

Rather than fitting any sort of cultural logic, the way Mukogodo parents favor their daughters appears to make the most sense in terms of evolutionary biology. It turns out that we humans are by no means the only species that adjusts its treatment of sons and daughters according to their life prospects; such an adaptation is quite widespread. Among spider monkeys, for example, the males stay with their mothers while female children disperse to other troops. This means that a mother's status can have an influence on her sons' success, but not on that of her daughters. And spider monkeys seem to have evolved to take advantage of this. High-status females give birth to about equal numbers of daughters and sons, but low-status females give birth only to daughters. High-status mothers also carry their sons longer than their daughters, and the interval after the birth of a male before another birth is longer than that following the birth of a female.[29] Given the apparent lack of a cultural reason for the way that Mukogodo parents favor their daughters, the most parsimonious explanation is that we humans, too, have an evolved capacity to adjust how we care for our sons and daughters according to their prospects.

The animal behavior literature is full of examples of behavioral diversity without culture. People not familiar with animal-behavior studies often assume that animals behave in narrow, rigidly programmed ways dictated by fixed instincts and that as a result their behavior varies little within any one species, but it has long been known that this is not true even for species that most people consider relatively primitive. For example, male scorpionflies have three different ways of getting a mate. They can either tempt a female with a nuptual gift of a dead insect, entice her with the somewhat less attractive gift of a glob of nutritious saliva secreted onto a leaf, or force a female to mate without offering anything nutritious in return. These are not fixed, separate strategies, but rather three tactics within one conditional strategy, as shown by the fact that male scorpionflies will switch to a more successful tactic when given an opportunity to do so.[30]

Both males and females of a European songbird called the dunnock also display a lot of variability in their mating strategies. Within a single population of dunnock, there may be monogamous pairs, polygynous arrangements, with one male mated to several females, polyandrous arrangements, with one female mated to several males, and even polygynandrous arrangements, in which males and females have multiple mates simultaneously, all depending on the distribution of food. When food is widely spread, females forage a greater territory, males have a hard time monopolizing them, and polyandry results. When females can find enough food without foraging so widely, monogamous and in extreme cases polygynous and polygynandrous unions occur.[31]

Among Florida scrub jays, behavioral variations occur not in mating systems but in helping behavior. A common pattern is for juvenile male jays to stay behind as helpers at their parents' nests, and it has been shown that this behavior does help the parents to raise more offspring. But when an opportunity opens up for the males to leave home and set up their own breeding territories, they take it.[32] Although as we saw in Chapter one it is by no means impossible for birds to have culture, there does not seem to be any reason to think that culture plays any role in any of these cases of behavioral diversity. In sum, there is no more reason to think that the mating strategies of scorpionflies, dunnocks, or Florida scrub jays are the products of culture than there is to think that Mukogodo favoritism toward daughters is one. Behavioral diversity by itself does not imply that culture is at work.

Human(izing) Nature

An objection many people have to these sorts of biological analyses of human behavior is that they are dehumanizing, even animalizing, and somehow alienate ourselves from ourselves. On the contrary, an emphasis on the evolved biological heritage we all as humans share can be quite humanizing: It helps us to see and appreciate the many things we have in common. Certainly there are some aspects of culture that are extraordinarily difficult to communicate to people with a different cultural background, but it is just as certain that there are enormous areas of the human experience that we all share because we are humans, all the same type of jukebox.

By the same token, an overemphasis on cultural differences can be dehumanizing and alienating. Witness, for example, the reaction of Samoan scholar Fanaafi Le Tagaloa to Margaret Mead's depiction of her people: "Margaret Mead took away our . . . oneness with other human beings. . . . We are no different from you in Australia or the United States or any other part of the world. . . . For Margaret Mead to make us behave as if we are nonhumans because we behave like animals in our promiscuity, I think that is a very great disfavor that she has done us."[33] Unfortunately, Mead is not the only cultural anthropologist who, for dramatic effect, has overemphasized the cultural differences that divide our species. For example, an otherwise excellent cultural anthropology textbook I recently reviewed featured in each chapter a box on "Cross-cultural miscues." These little stories told students about how incredibly difficult cross-cultural communication can be, ranging from amusing anecdotes about variations in the meanings of hand gestures and in business etiquette across cultures to tragic stories such as the Japanese exchange student who was shot by a Louisiana home owner who feared a break-in when the student failed to "freeze" as told (he may have thought the man said "please") and the Nestlé company's advertising of infant formula to women with access only to contaminated water. Even I have sometimes emphasized—and perhaps over-emphasized—cross-cultural differences for dramatic effect. In fact, one of the "cross-cultural miscues" featured in the textbook is borrowed from an article of mine about gift-giving. It explains how the derogatory phrase "Indian giver" may have originated from a misunderstanding among European settlers in the Americas of the Native American's gift-giving practices.[34] Unfortunately, not many of the textbook's examples of cross-cultural misunderstandings contained any information about how these problems can be and routinely are overcome, often with the help of cultural anthropologists. Instead, student readers may be left with the impression that the differences among the world's peoples are truly enormous and nearly impossible to bridge. Finally, this century's many "experiments" in social engineering demonstrate the dehumanizing power of the notion that all human behavior is the result of learning, and the resounding failure of those experiments helps prove the falsity of this premise.

Another fear, equally unfounded, is that biology is destiny. Even if this were true—and I don't think it is—what choice would we have but to study our evolved propensities even more diligently and carefully than we now do? Surely, the only way we will ever be able to be free is to understand what we are as biological and cultural beings. Only then can we make intelligent, informed choices about the directions we want our lives and our societies to take. In the area of reproduction—so central to humans and Gethenians alike—what changes might we make if given the chance, and what effects might those changes have on the broader social and cultural patterns that arise from the details of our reproductive process? Actually, this is not the stuff of science fiction. Radical changes in the way people reproduce are already with us. Breast feeding, though for many reasons preferable to bottle-feeding, is now strictly speaking unnecessary, and sexual intercourse itself can also now be bypassed through *in vitro* fertilization. Surrogate motherhood is a first step in separating a mother from her developing fetus, and artificial wombs will complete the move.

Given that it is now possible to clone mammals, some day soon not only intercourse but even fertilization may be avoidable as scientists invent ways for women to reproduce without the help of sperm. As the technology of reproduction improves, eventually women might decide that males are actually little more than vestiges of an evolutionary history in which sexual reproduction was an advantage, of as little relevance to modern reproductive life as the appendix is to modern digestion.[35]

Perhaps a race of asexually reproducing females would eventually want to reinvent heterosexual intercourse, if for no other reason than as an enjoyable pastime. But it seems unlikely that they would redivide the world into male and female, and this brings us back to Gethen. Interestingly, our ethnographer friend O. T. Oppong speculates that Gethenian sexual physiology was the product of genetic engineering. The thing to remember is that although human nature may be worthy of more attention and respect than most social scientists now give it, even in the absence of genetic engineering, biology is not destiny. Understanding our evolved propensities does not shackle us to our evolutionary roots, it frees us to find our way through ethnographic hyperspace, where we may well choose to go where no one has gone before.

3

The Blob

In the animal ovum, as well as in the seed of a plant, we recognise a certain
remarkable force, the source of growth, or increase in the mass, and of
reproduction, or of supply of the matter consumed; a force in a state of
rest. . . . This force is called the vital force, vis vitae, or vitality.

—Justus Liebig[1]

Culture is a thing sui generis which can be explained only in terms of itself.
This is not mysticism but sound scientific method. . . . So the ethnologist
will do well to postulate the principle, Omnia cultura ex cultura.

—Robert Lowie[2]

A Frightening Prospect

Not long ago, all scholars were considered "philosophers," literally "lovers of
knowledge." Strict divisions between disciplines did not exist. The same person might work one day in what we now call physics, the next day write up
some observations on plants, and the next day speculate on social organization. This renaissance man idea is preserved in the name we give to our highest academic degree, "Doctor of Philosophy."

These days, of course, all scholars are not "philosophers." Instead, we have
physicists, mathematicians, anthropologists, and so on. As we learn more
and more about particular topics, they break away from the vast, daunting
subject matter called philosophy and develop into disciplines of their own.
Some of this is simply the result of specialization in all aspects of our society

39

over the past millennium, but much is because of the enormous improvements in human knowledge produced by the sciences. Bertrand Russell succinctly summarized this intellectual division of labor between the sciences and philosophy when he wrote, "Roughly, science is what we know and philosophy is what we don't know."[3] As science has come to know more and more, less and less has been included under the heading of "philosophy."

The ever-expanding, ever-improving body of knowledge produced by the sciences is to human ignorance what "The Blob" was to small towns in cheesy horror movies. From Galileo's simple physics, the blob that is scientific knowledge has expanded relentlessly, touching and absorbing field after field until almost nothing is left outside. What remains to be absorbed is, chiefly, the study of human behavior, social patterns, and culture. Is absorption by "The Blob" something to be feared or something to be accepted and encouraged?

For social and behavioral scientists, certainly, the blob is a frightening thing. This was made clear more than twenty years ago when Harvard biologist E. O. Wilson published *Sociobiology: The New Synthesis*.[4] Wilson, an entomologist, documented the tremendous progress made since the 1960s in the use of evolutionary biological theory to study animal behavior, particularly social behaviors such as communication, mating, parenting, territoriality, and the formation of dominance hierarchies. Although the middle twenty-five of *Sociobiology*'s twenty-seven chapters were nothing more (or less) than a masterful and exhaustive textbook on the study of animal social behavior, the first and last chapters, "The Morality of the Gene" and "Man: From Sociobiology to Sociology" were received by social scientists with such fear and loathing that one would have thought the blob truly was on the rampage. This reaction was understandable. In the first chapter, Wilson suggested that "it may not be too much to say that sociology and the other social sciences, as well as the humanities, are the last branches of biology waiting to be included in the Modern Synthesis. One of the functions of sociobiology, then, is to reformulate the foundations of the social sciences in a way that draws these subjects into the Modern Synthesis." The impression that a menacing blob was on the doorstep was not helped by Wilson's inclusion in the first chapter of a set of diagrams depicting the development of the blob over time. These diagrams showed how since the 1950s such fields as ethology and comparative psychology had been absorbed and transformed by contact with sociobiology, neurophysiology, and behavioral ecology.

Combine Wilson's imperialistic statements and his diagram of the blob in action, its lobes extending and absorbing hapless disciplines like an amoeba, and it is easy to see how they generated such a reaction at the time. Sociologists, anthropologists, psychologists, and others who had spent their entire careers teaching and doing research on subjects they considered their rightful intellectual territory in complete and, in their view, completely justifiable ignorance of biology were suddenly being told that their property had been bought out from under them, and that they were being evicted. Those who jumped on the sociobiology bandwagon had an aggravating tendency to rub salt in the wound by declaring, as did one philosopher of science, that the social sciences had not only "failed," but that they were being "replaced, superseded, preempted, by sociobiology."[5]

Occasionally, the alarm of the social sciences over these imperialistic claims has led to surprisingly defensive and quite unscientific behavior. Consider, for example, the treatment Derek Freeman of the Australian National University received when, in a 1982 book titled *Margaret Mead and Samoa: The Making and Unmaking of an Anthropological Myth,*[6] he argued against Margaret Mead's portrayal of Samoan adolescence and in favor of an approach to culture that takes seriously our species' shared, evolved human nature. Mead, you will recall from Chapter 2, went to Samoa in the 1920s at the behest of her mentor, Franz Boas of Columbia University, and came back with the news that Samoans demonstrated that how one experiences adolescence is culturally determined and highly flexible. And if that aspect of life is culturally determined, so the argument went, so must be the rest of human life.

Considering his own work in Samoa, Freeman argued that Samoan adolescence, far from the free and easy time described by Mead, is not that different from adolescence anywhere else in the world. Understandably, anthropologists did not take kindly to anyone criticizing someone who had been so important to the development and success of their discipline. Their rancor toward Freeman was described in a resolution passed at the 1983 annual meeting of the American Anthropological Association characterizing his book as "poorly written, unscientific, irresponsible and misleading."[7] It was not until four years later that Freeman was vindicated when one of Mead's key informants came forward with the news that she and her friends "just fibbed and fibbed" to the young fieldworker, leaving the American Anthropological Association looking rather foolish (see Chapter 2).[8]

It is not that social scientists were afraid of the idea of science itself or scientific methods. Although it has recently become the "postmodern" fashion to declare science either dead on arrival or irrelevant to an understanding of our own species, twenty years ago the vast majority of social and behavioral scientists took it for granted that the development of a true science of human behavior, society, and culture was the Holy Grail toward which they were striving. Accordingly, anthropologists of that time routinely patterned their studies after those of the established sciences, developing theories about human behavior, society, and culture, and conducting rigorous and quantitative tests of various hypotheses. Yet, the advent of sociobiology made it clear to many that it was no longer enough for social scientists to act like their colleagues in the natural sciences. It was also necessary to link the study of behavior with the study of all other phenomena in the universe, and that meant using biology as the intellectual connective tissue.

What Is Science?

Science, of course, is a type of social discourse and a sort of culture. Although this kind of thing is often said to denigrate science, to remove the specialness of its claims to knowledge compared to those claimed by, say, the humanities or religions, in fact the statement does no such thing. As long as science is conducted by people and for people, it will always be a sort of discourse and a cultural tradition. But that does not put it on a par with ancestor worship. Science's claims to knowledge truly are special because they are self-correcting and so, in the long run, tend toward improvement. This makes scientific knowledge different from, say, knowledge in the arts or the humanities. Knowledge in the arts and humanities may develop and expand, but we cannot say that it really "improves." While twentieth-century art or music is not clearly "better" than eighteenth-century art or music, twentieth-century chemistry is many, many times better than eighteenth-century chemistry. The knowledge of chemistry contained in a contemporary highschool textbook on the subject far exceeds that of even the best practitioners of the discipline of two centuries ago. In the arts and humanities, in contrast to the sciences, the goal is not to expand and refine our understanding of the workings of the universe in which we find ourselves, but rather to produce things of beauty and meaning and to understand the significance they have for people.

Although the details of what exactly constitutes a science are debated endlessly by philosophers and by scientists themselves, as a practical matter the notion at the core of all scientific inquiry is testability. A statement is not scientific unless it is testable, and for a statement to be testable it must, as the philosopher of science Karl Popper pointed out, be falsifiable—it must be possible to imagine a set of data that could prove the statement wrong.[9] Popper grew up in the lively intellectual milieu of Vienna early in the twentieth century. As with many of his contemporaries, he was initially impressed with the popular theories of the time, particularly Marxism and Freudianism. Everywhere one looked, from the events in the newspapers to one's dreams, one could find apparent confirmations of those theories, which thus appear at first glance to be spectacularly successful. Indeed, nothing could be imagined that could prove them wrong, and so they seemed to be absolutely right.

However, another theory being widely discussed at the time, Einstein's theory of relativity, was, Popper sensed, somehow different. Confirmations of the theory of relativity were hardly abundant. On the contrary, the theory made some rather surprising and outlandish predictions, even going so far as to stick its neck out and declare certain things to be absolutely impossible. One of its most original predictions was that gravity should be able to bend light. Previous theories held, in contrast, that light moved undisturbed through the ether of space, unperturbed by gravity. The most massive nearby object is the sun, and so, if Einstein was right, from our point of view the sun should bend the light of the stars behind it, making them appear to be in places in the sky other than where they appear in the night sky. Unfortunately, during the daytime this is normally impossible to test because the brightness of the sun blots out the feeble light of the stars behind it. But during a solar eclipse the sun is momentarily darkened and the stars become visible. Measurements taken during an eclipse in 1919 made it clear that Einstein was right: Gravity really does bend light. Since that time, astronomers have detected many examples of light bending by gravity, including so-called gravitational lenses, in which a very massive object distorts our picture of the objects that lie beyond it, creating multiple images of certain galaxies. Had Einstein's prediction been proved wrong, then the entire structure of his theory would have collapsed. Similarly, several decades before Popper was born Charles Darwin wrote, "If it could be proved that any part of the structure of any one species had been formed for the exclusive good of another species, it would annihilate my theory, for such could not have been produced through natural selection."[10] Marxism and Freudianism, in contrast, make no such risky predictions, claiming instead to be able to explain virtually anything that might happen in society or in someone's head, and hence are not *scientific* theories at all.

Once a proposition has been stated in a scientific way—that is, as a falsifiable hypothesis—it can be tested. If it passes that test, it can then be considered "scientific knowledge." But "scientific knowledge" is a special type of knowledge different from the everyday use of the word. At least in spirit, all scientific knowledge, even things we think we know beyond a shadow of a doubt, is tentative. All claims to scientific knowledge are at least potentially subject to additional tests. Why accept tentative knowledge when others offer absolute knowledge? Because it is only by accepting the tentativeness of scientific knowledge that we gain the promise science holds out to us: an ever-improving and ever-expanding understanding of the universe around us. Science asks us to strike this bargain: Give up the goal of absolute knowledge, accept the permanent tentativeness of all scientific propositions, and in exchange it will give you a steadily improving understanding of the way things work. This is not a perfect method, and it is as subject to failures and foibles as anything humans do, but it is the best way we have and probably the best we will ever have of learning about our universe.

Types of Science

Although there is broad agreement that testability is the core of the scientific method, beyond that there is disagreement and confusion about what constitutes a "science." In particular there is a tendency to assume that if a field cannot mimic the structure and methods of the "hard" sciences, such as physics, conducting experiments and producing "laws," then it cannot be a science. But many fields that are widely accepted as sciences, such as geology, oceanography, and astronomy, do no such thing. A useful distinction is between what are sometimes called "theoretical" or "Newtonian" sciences and "historical" ones. The "Newtonian" or "theoretical" sciences deal with general rules of general phenomena, like the behavior of elementary particles, chemical reactions, or the laws of genetic inheritance. Historical sciences, on the other hand, do not seek such broad principles, but instead use the insights of the theoretical sciences to explain the specifics of local, particular situations. The late Austrian economist and Nobel laureate Friedrich Hayek[11] clarified this distinction by comparing the method of the historical sciences to the way you would go about a systematic and scientific study of the way that a garden fills up with weeds. You would have to carefully record all of the changes in the plot and learn the details about different sorts of soil in different parts of the plot, different amounts of sunlight and shade in different places, and so on. To make sense of your data, you would need to borrow theory from a variety of fields, including physics, chemistry, and biology. This is essentially what geologists, astronomers, and other historical scientists must do: Carefully record complex phenomena and attempt to make sense of them using ideas borrowed from the theoretical sciences. Most social scientists are in the same position, faced with an enormous complexity of things to study, each one of which is the product of nearly countless influences, some immeasurably small, some so large they're obvious to everyone, and many others frustratingly in between. To understand any particular thing in human behavior, social organization, or culture, we need to bring to bear the insights provided by a variety of other disciplines. Social scientists may never have the aesthetic pleasure theoretical physicists get from reducing everything to the basic forces of nature through simple and elegant equations, but they are still as capable as any physicist of being a scientist and doing science.

Waiting to Be Normal

If the social sciences are capable of becoming true sciences in this sense and if most social scientists have, at least traditionally, supported this as a major goal, then why has it generally not been accomplished? Historian of science Thomas Kuhn suggested one possible and popular answer: Perhaps science, like some other aspects of culture, develops in stages, with some sciences passing through the stages of development or maturation more quickly than others.[12] Kuhn referred to a mature science as a "normal" one, meaning that it has reached a stage in which its practitioners share a basic paradigm that guides their research, leading them to consider some sorts of questions and problems to be significant and others trivial. Because they all share a common framework and vocabulary, practitioners of the normal sciences can take a lot for granted when they write, and so the short scientific article tends to be the main way they share their findings.

Sciences that are not yet "normal" in the Kuhnian sense have not developed a shared paradigm. These sciences are typified by dissent, disagreement, and diversity among practitioners. Researchers pursue their ideas and agendas, collecting data and building up cases for their favorite theories and ideas. Because the researchers do not share a paradigm, they do not share a vocabulary, and so their written products during the prescience period tend to be long affairs, including lengthy explanations of the basics of their particular approach. Physics before Newton is a classic example. People like Francis Bacon, for instance, who lived at the time of Shakespeare, compiled enormous amounts of data on a variety of physical phenomena, but with no clear guide as to what might be important and what might be trivial. After the advent of a Newton as in physics, a Ben Franklin as in the study of electricity, or a Darwin as in biology, on the other hand, communication is mainly in brief, technical articles because everyone shares the same broad concepts and vocabulary.

Many have argued that the social sciences are still prescientific, amassing a wealth of data on a variety of topics because they do not have a clear idea of what is important. Henry Harpending, an anthropologist at the University of Utah, has humorously illustrated this prescientific quality of the social sciences by asking us to imagine what chemistry would be like if it were approached using the techniques of the social sciences:

> We would spend a lot of money measuring anything measurable about substances and materials around us. With modern computers, we would create a huge database; with modern software, we would make any patterns readily apparent. We would discover, for example, a correlation between "conducts electricity" and "shininess." In the jargon we would say that "shininess" is a determinant of conducting electricity. Another group would find that "density" is also a determinant of conducting electricity. Papers would appear discussing whether density is a determinant of shininess or shininess of density. None of this would get us close to the periodic table or anywhere near modern chemistry. Meanwhile policy experts would advocate polishing household machinery to make it shinier, and thus more efficient. Universities would be plagued with workshops on shining up things.[13]

This is indeed not all that far from how the physical sciences really were conducted before breakthroughs by people like Newton and Franklin. The obvious implication of this analogy for the social sciences, of course, is that what they need is for a genius—a Darwin of the social sciences, if you will—to come along to set things right.

Making Connections

There is certainly something to this interpretation, and it is what I have taught in classrooms for many years. Yet, recently I have come to the conclusion that even though the social sciences, like virtually all fields, could use some more brilliant people, they alone will not transform the social sciences into "normal" sciences. For that to happen, the same thing needs to happen that has happened to every other field in science: They first need to become connected to the blob.[14]

The social sciences' resistance to being linked with the rest of the sciences is not surprising or new. The same sort of resistance has been met every time that the expanding body of scientific knowledge threatened (or promised, depending on your point of view) to touch on some new topic. The pattern is always roughly the same. Before the absorption, a variety of reasons are given why absorption is impossible, why science as we know it has finally reached its limit, why the principles and concepts that have worked in other sciences just won't work in this new area. Perhaps the most spectacular example of the strength of this notion and its eventual demise was in biology, where for centuries two opposing camps battled over the question of whether the study of living things can be incorporated into the existing sciences at all, or whether life involved processes so radically different from anything in physics or chemistry that biological knowledge must always remain unconnected to the rest of scientific knowledge. On one side were the mechanists, who argued that living things are essentially machines and can be understood the same way that we would understand, say, a locomotive, by direct application of the laws of chemistry and physics. To the mechanists, there is fundamentally nothing different about living things. Rocks and gophers both, after all, must obey the same law of gravity, must be subject to inertia, must have a temperature, and so on. The mechanists asked the naive but important question, what's the big deal about life? On the other side were the vitalists. To them, living things were quite a big deal, and different from nonliving things. What made them distinct was some ineffable thing known as "vital force" or simply "vitality." For vitalists, this special essence was what made living things different from nonliving things, and it is what makes them "go." Vital force was thought of as something beyond mere physics and chemistry, something not necessarily beholden to those fields' supposed "laws."

This notion of vital force can still be found in folk biology—I can't count the number of episodes of *Star Trek* I have watched in which some nasty alien is said to have the power to suck the very "life force" out of people—but it is virtually dead among biologists themselves. Its demise came with increasing understanding of biochemistry, such as the laboratory synthesis of urea and other chemicals formerly found only in living things, which demystified life and made it clear that there is no reason to posit the existence of such a "force" to explain living things. But that does not mean that all biologists are now mechanists, simply treating organisms as complicated machines. There *is* something special about living things, but it is not "vital force." This specialness, this understanding that, while living things have to obey the laws of physics and chemistry, they cannot be explained with only those laws, is best captured by the idea of "emergence." Emergence refers to the fact that, sometimes, bigger or more complex is not just bigger or more complex, it is also *different*. Living things are not just machines, but they aren't imbued with any mystical force, either. They are different from nonliving things because they have crossed a threshold beyond which they develop properties that cannot be explained simply through an understanding of the physics and chemistry involved, properties like the way individual organisms develop and the way that species evolve through natural selection.

Emergence itself can sound rather mystical at first, until we realize that it is an everyday thing. The difference between nonliving and living things is one example of emergence, but it is by no means the only one. Even something as simple as water displays emergence in the sense that one could not predict water's properties based on a knowledge of its components, oxygen and hydrogen. Within physics, the laws of thermodynamics are now understood to emerge from the behavior of fundamental particles and forces. That understanding, like the battle between the mechanists and vitalists in biology, was also the result of a hard-fought struggle between the statistical mechanics, who advocated an explanation of thermodynamics as something emergent, and those who argued that the laws of thermodynamics were somehow independent and separate from what went on among individual atoms and molecules.[15]

If thermodynamics, the chemical properties of elements, and biology are all emergent, then clearly emergence doesn't prevent or forestall scientific methods or understanding. The lesson for the social sciences in all of this is clear: On the one hand, there are indeed perfectly good reasons for thinking that there is something special, something not just more complex but truly *different*, about human society and culture. Human social patterns and cultural traditions are not just the sum totals of the behaviors of individuals, they are something more, something emergent. Indeed, it is fairly routine in human societies for institutions and customs to arise from the interactions of individuals without anyone foreseeing or planning them. These "spontaneous orders" can be explained using "invisible-hand" models, the most famous of which is, of course, Adam Smith's classic explanation of how the order of the market system emerges without planning from the small-scale interactions of individuals going about their business with no attention to the overall pattern. Consider how money probably first developed through the interactions of individuals without anyone deliberately planning it: First there is only barter, then some people notice that some goods are easier to exchange than others and engage in triangular exchanges to take advantage of this, trading for something they don't really want because they can use it to get something they do want. When one good emerges as having greater "currency" than any other because of its usefulness as a means of exchange, we call it money. It is only later that money comes to be deliberately designed as a means of exchange by banks and governments.[16] On the other hand, these things and many others are indeed emergent, and for that reason they cannot be truly separate from the actions of the individuals. While an understanding of them would not be forthcoming from an examination of the intentions of any one individual in the system, we do need to understand the individuals' intentions, at least in broad outline, if we are to understand why things like market systems, money, or cultural traditions emerge in the first place.

Culture Emergent

The hubris of the sociobiologists in the 1970s was to suggest that they could absorb and even preempt the social sciences without first taking into account what really is special about human society and culture. They asserted that social organization and culture are nothing more than the sum total of the behavior of individuals, which can be explained using notions from evolutionary biology. In that sense they were like the mechanists, asserting that what seems to be so different about life, society, or culture is really not different at all. Sometimes they even sounded like the mechanists, going so far as to refer to humans and other organisms as "survival machines" for genes.[17] The vitalists in this story are, of course, the vast majority of social scientists, who for years had been and still are arguing that there is indeed something almost ineffably special about society and culture, something that puts them in a separate category from all other phenomena known to science—something that makes other sciences, including biology, not just inadequate to explain them, but fundamentally irrelevant to an understanding of them. To them, "Culture is a thing *sui generis*. . . . *Omnia cultura ex cultura*."[18] Even more starkly, Emile Durkheim, a tremendously influential sociologist of the late nineteenth and early twentieth centuries, put it this way: "Every time that a social phenomenon is directly explained by a psychological phenomenon, we may be sure that the explanation is false."[19]

Over the years, this belief in the distinctiveness and separateness of culture has hardened to the point that at times it appears to rest more on faith than on reason. One cultural anthropologist recently argued, for example, that "culture patterns provide the template for *all* human action, growth and understanding," and "culture does not dictate simply *what* we think but how we feel about and live our lives."[20] Anthropologists' writings about culture sometimes take on an almost quasi-religious quality. For example, when one cultural anthropologist was asked by a Muslim group in Indonesia, "What is your religion?" he replied, "My religion is anthropology." That same anthropologist also compares the experience of conducting anthropological fieldwork to "the conversion experience in which, to use a phrase popularized by fundamentalist Christianity, one is 'born again.' Like Saul on the road to Damascus, like Augustine or Martin Luther, the convert experiences a dramatic transformation; the scales fall from his eyes, he sees the world anew; in fact, he lives in a new world, for he is born again, a new person."[21] For some, the importance of culture in human affairs is no longer a hypothesis to be tested, but a power to be witnessed. An increasingly popular view of the purpose of ethnographies is not to look at a variety of influences on behavior but rather to be an advocate for just one influence, culture, and "to persuade the reader that culture matters more than he might have thought."[22]

As in biology, where an appreciation of the emergent properties of living things spelled the end of mechanism and vitalism, an understanding of how social and cultural phenomena are emergent properties of humans living together and interacting with each other lays to rest any claim that social and cultural phenomena exist somehow outside the rest of the sciences, outside the blob of our expanding scientific understanding of the universe, while recognizing that society and culture do have properties that cannot be explained or predicted simply from an understanding of biology. This repeats a process that has occurred over and over throughout the history of the sciences showing that no scientific knowledge is really outside the blob. For example, Galileo, Kepler, and Newton's work showed that the motions of the planets were governed by the same forces that govern falling objects here on earth, breaking down the formerly sacred division between the celestial and terrestrial realms, while the great geologist Charles Lyell's doctrine of gradualism destroyed the distinction between the seemingly static present and the formative past.[23]

A scientific understanding of the universe is a continuous, connected thing. Making sense out of any phenomenon requires, fundamentally, connecting it somehow with the rest of what we understand. Where there is emergence, the connections become particularly complex, interesting, and challenging, but they are always present nonetheless. The reason why the social sciences have stayed separate from the rest of the sciences for so long is not for lack of a Newton or Darwin to lay things straight with a powerful paradigm, but because the blob of science had not yet reached them. It was not so much that the social sciences were not ready to be sciences, but rather that science was not ready for the social sciences. It had not reached the point where it could shed any light on the many complex and vexing problems uncovered by social scientists in their studies of human behavior, society, and culture.

Forming Texts

The latest attempt to erect a Great Wall between science and the study of culture has come in the name of "postmodernism." Because their critique of the possibility of creating a science of culture is insightful and influential, it is worth spending some time explaining why it is also, fundamentally, wrong.

Postmodernism has taken many forms, often bearing little resemblance to one another. In my field of cultural anthropology, one major thrust of the postmodernist movement has come in the form of what I like to call the "We are not worthy!" argument for the distinctiveness of the study of culture. A more popular name for it, and possibly even a better one, is the "textualist" critique of ethnography.[24] The basic argument goes like this: Sciences depend on clear-cut, objectively measured data. The data anthropologists have to work with, on the other hand, come to them in the form of ethnographic texts, which are so inherently subjective, full of personal interpretations, complex, and biased that it is virtually impossible to use them for any sort of scientific purpose. We are forced, therefore, to abandon the goal of building a science of culture and must instead pursue a humanistic understanding of it.[25]

At the root of the textualist argument is a misunderstanding about the nature of science. The scientific status of cultural anthropology does not depend—nor did it ever depend—on the authority of ethnographic texts. What makes a field a science is not to be found in the way it collects its basic data but rather in the way in which it phrases questions, tests them, and makes claims to new knowledge. Astronomy, for example, is definitely a science, but not because astronomers have sophisticated equipment and make careful observations of the heavens. Astronomy is a science because of how astronomers decide which problems to address, how they phrase those problems, and how they relate their data to them. Research priorities of astronomy and other sciences are typically set by a dominant paradigm, questions typically are expected to be phrased as falsifiable hypotheses, and researchers attempt to relate data to hypotheses using methods that are fairly standard. If we suddenly took away from the world's astronomers all of their sophisticated observatories and gave them instead to their anti-scientific counterparts in astrology, the astronomers would not become something other than scientists and the astrologers certainly would not become scientists. Chances are, the astronomers would continue their struggle for knowledge, unaided by anything other than the naked eye, while the astrologers would simply incorporate previously invisible objects like the planets beyond Saturn, quasars, pulsars, and nebulae into their nonscientific and mystical belief system.

Similarly, the scientific status of cultural anthropology rests not on how ethnographers collect their data and write up their findings, but rather on the way those hypotheses are derived, the way they are phrased, and the way they are tested. Scientists in cultural anthropology's sister discipline of archaeology have recently had to grapple with a similar problem, and it may be helpful to take a quick look at how they handled it. The data that archaeologists have to work with are, like ethnographic texts, fraught with problems. What's left behind when people abandon a place may not be the most important for reconstructing their way of life, not all materials preserve equally well when buried by sediment, burrowing animals can change the way artifacts are arranged in the soil, sometimes materials from archaeological sites are reused again and again, complicating their interpretation, and so on. In the 1960s, these sources of bias in the archaeological record became known as "archaeological site formation processes."[26] When archaeologists began to appreciate the problems created for them by such processes, it is worth noting what they did not do. They did not throw up their hands and declare that because archaeological sites are messy places created by a variety of forces that are difficult to reconstruct we must abandon all hope for a science of the past. On the contrary, they redoubled and refocused their efforts to understand how the archaeological record was created and what it says about our ancestors, their societies, and their cultures. This led to a new appreciation of the details of site formation, including new research on the geology of archaeological sites and the ways in which humans create sites through their behavior.

To continue this analogy with archaeology, what the textualists are asking for is essentially an understanding of "ethnographic text formation processes"—the ways in which bits and pieces of the behavior and statements of people around the world get enshrined in ethnographic texts.[27] Ironically, pursuing the textualists' agenda is exactly what we should do to further our quest for a science of culture. Just as an archaeologist needs a thorough understanding of how archaeological sites are created and an astronomer needs to know how the atmosphere and the characteristics of his telescope distort his observations of the stars, so must cultural anthropologists appreciate the complexities and subtleties of ethnographic text formation. Clearly, some ethnographic field methods enable us to make more solid knowledge claims than others. A cross-cultural analysis based only on the reports of individuals with long residence in the societies in question and good knowledge of the local languages involved will provide more reliable findings than one based only on, say, travelers' reports. Indeed, it has been shown that the longer an ethnographer spends in the field, the more likely he or she is to report the existence of witchcraft, and the same is probably true of other hidden and otherwise hard to detect customs and beliefs.

The question becomes, then, what sorts of field methods and ways of writing ethnography contribute more, and which contribute less, to the development of a science of culture? On this issue the jury is largely still out. An encouraging sign, though, is a new spirit of openness and experimentation that imbues current ethnography. For example, there has recently been a great deal of attention paid to the rather mundane and normally quite private business of ethnographers' field notes.[28] Until recently, anthropologists' attitude toward field notes has been rather like men in a locker room: The polite thing is not to stare, and certainly one never asks for a peek. The whole topic engenders a certain self-consciousness and doubt about the adequacy of one's own fieldwork. But now ethnographers are taking steps to share their field notes, discussing openly how they collected them and sometimes even including them in their publications. Doing this may make it possible to reconstruct what is sometimes called "the life history of a fact":[29] How an idea begins in the field with an observation or an informant's statement and then grows until it is eventually enshrined in an ethnographic text.

My work on the Mukogodo can provide a simple example of how observations and informants' statements find their way into ethnographic texts. My writings on the Mukogodo are typical of most ethnography in the sense that they are full of simple declarative statements about their culture. For example, I have often written that "the Mukogodo are patrilineal." But what exactly does that mean, and how do I know it to be true? What it means is that the Mukogodo have a patrilineal-descent system formed from descent groups, called clans and lineages, and that to be a member of such a group one is supposed to have all male links back to the group's male founding ancestor. For the vast majority of Mukogodo individuals, this is indeed true. They identify themselves with a particularly large descent group called a clan and a smaller group called a lineage. A person gains membership in these groups only through male links: his father, his father's father, and so on. I know this because I carefully collected genealogies of all thirteen Mukogodo lineages they contain in about twenty long interviews, mostly with older Mukogodo men. Considering those interviews, I can assert with confidence that if you were to pick a Mukogodo individual at random, he or she would very probably be able to trace his or her lineage and clan identification through male links back to a male founding ancestor. I can also tell you that this may not be the case for everybody. Sometimes, for instance when a woman has children in her father's name without ever marrying, a person can be a member of a Mukogodo descent group without having any male link to it. Understanding that such complexities and caveats are likely to be behind virtually everything included in ethnographies is a first step toward being able to use them critically to develop a science of culture.

Developing an appreciation of the technical details of ethnographic text formation will not in any way detract from the more humanistic goals of tex-tualist and postmodernist anthropologists. Their approach has already sparked a veritable renaissance in the field of ethnographic writing, fostering the creation of a new, refreshing, sensitive, and unashamedly subjective style of ethnography. These new ethnographies go more for the reader's heart than for his mind, breaking through barriers to cross-cultural understanding with emotionally evocative descriptions of real people rather than through ratio-nal analysis of their behavior and beliefs. This style of ethnographic writing can and should exist alongside a new scientific approach to culture in the same way that a rich body of literature on the wonders of nature has grown alongside our rapidly expanding technical, scientific understanding of life on Earth. Indeed, many of the best nature writers are themselves serious profes-sional biologists, and it is to be hoped that we who study humans are able to emulate them.

Connectionism, Reductionism, and Unity

The idea of the "unity of the sciences" has a long history, and it may be worth taking a moment to clarify what I am and am not saying. The phrase "Unity of Science" is associated most closely with a group of positivist philosophers of science earlier in this century known as the "Vienna Circle," which included the famous physicist Niels Bohr. Along with such English speakers as John Dewey and Bertrand Russell, the Vienna Circle organized and contributed to something called the "International Encyclopedia of Uni-fied Science." Those scholars were committed to a particular sort of unifica-tion of the sciences that is different from the connectionism I am advocating. To advocates of the "unity of science," as opposed to advocates of "the unity of scientific knowledge" like me, ultimately the subject matter of every discipline was to be translated into the framework of physics, and laws for all things, from atoms to language to social organization, were to be derived from the principles of physics. Whether this is desirable or even possible is something on which I am more or less agnostic, but in any case it is not what I am proposing. The idea that all sciences are connected to one another does not necessarily imply that any science can be completely reduced to another in this sense or that any science is any more fundamental than any other. What would be a quark-level explanation of the nepotistic human tendency to favor kin over non-kin? I don't know, and I doubt the answer, if there is one, would tell us anything interesting. But linking the study of human social behavior, including nepotism, with the rest of the sciences does indeed provide great insights into why people tend to favor their closest relatives.

Nor does this connectionistic view of scientific knowledge necessarily extend to other forms of knowledge. The idea that all forms of knowledge may one day be seamlessly connected has been espoused recently by E. O. Wilson under the label "consilience."[30] In many ways Wilson's arguments in favor of consilience are much like my arguments in favor of connecting the studies of behavior, society, and culture to the rest of our scientific knowledge. This is to be expected given the influence that Wilson's other work has had on my own thinking and the fact that he and I are working from similar premises and assumptions. But Wilson goes far beyond my limited and somewhat timid (despite my horror film rhetoric) connectionism and argues that one day all forms of human knowledge, including not only scientific knowledge but also the humanities, arts, and even ethics and religion (more on that in Chapter 7) will be linked. He may well be right, but at any rate his argument and the one I am making here are not the same. My interest at this point is solely in expanding the bounds of scientific knowledge and scientific discourse, not encouraging science to encroach on fields where it is not welcome and very well may not belong.

The blob's expansion, mind you, is a horizontal affair, not a vertical one. Linking sciences together and applying scientific methods and theories to new areas does not mean that those newly incorporated areas are somehow subordinate to long-standing sciences. Physics does not trump biology, and biology does not trump sociology. A dramatic illustration of this principle came in the nineteenth century, when physicists posed a serious challenge to Darwin's theory of gradual evolution through natural selection. For Darwin's theory to be right, the earth had to be quite old. After all, life had to have time to get from its simplest beginnings to the complex organisms we see today, and even with a powerful mechanism like natural selection driving it, that would take time.

The physicists, though, would not give it time. As far as they could tell, the earth simply was not old enough for Darwin's process to be able to explain life as we know it. Among the leading skeptics was a man born in 1824 as William Thomson but who, thanks to a peerage granted him in 1894 by Queen Victoria, became known to posterity as Lord Kelvin. Kelvin, the co-discoverer of the second law of thermodynamics whose name has been given to the temperature scale that begins with absolute zero, estimated the Earth's age by looking at its present temperature and extrapolating backwards on the assumption that it must have started off hot and been cooling ever since. As he gained new knowledge and changed crucial assumptions throughout his career, Kelvin changed his estimates, which ranged from a high of 400 million years to a low of 20 million, settling late in his career on the lower figure. Turning to the sun, Kelvin estimated that if its heat came from the effects of smaller bodies colliding with one another and if it, like the earth, has been cooling ever since it was formed, then it could be no older than half a billion years.

What Kelvin did not know about was radioactivity, on the one hand, and nuclear fusion, on the other. As scientists early in this century figured out quickly after the discovery of radioactivity, the constant radioactive decay of elements within the Earth makes it hotter than it otherwise would be, therefore making it appear to be younger than it really is to people relying solely on a knowledge of thermodynamics. The sun is much older than Kelvin thought because it is powered not by rocks colliding, but by hydrogen nuclei fusing. In short, the biologist Darwin was right and the physicist Kelvin was wrong.[31] As new areas become incorporated with the blob, there is every reason to think that the social sciences' knowledge and theories will challenge accepted notions in the natural sciences, including evolutionary biology.

First Contact

SWEET AND SASSY Attractive, educated, fit single white professional female, seeking fit, attractive, intelligent, secure non-smoking single white professional male, 35–42, with honor and substance, for possible long term relationship.

DEGREED PROFESSIONAL Attractive single white male, 36, 6', fit, athletic, never married. Seeking attractive, fit, outgoing SWF, with similar interests, for possible long term relationship.[1]

Pigeons and Goats

If the last chapter was about The Blob, then this chapter is about The Tentacle: that part of the sciences that in recent years has reached out, touched, and begun to connect the study of human behavior to the rest of our scientific knowledge. Although the application of evolutionary theory to the study of our species goes back to Darwin, until recently it was mainly limited to the study of our physical characteristics—how we developed such big brains, how we developed the ability to walk upright, how we developed the ability to grasp things with our opposable thumb, and so on. Over the past few decades, however, a new group of researchers has begun to ask questions about the evolution of human behavior. This new approach, involving anthropologists such as me as well as psychologists, sociologists, economists, and political scientists, explores whether evolutionary theory can shed light not only on our species' striking physical characteristics, but on the way we behave and how we think.[2] Consider, for example, the "personals" or "lonely hearts" advertisements at the beginning of the chapter. They clearly show us something of sociological interest about our society: A lot of people have a hard time finding suitable mates. Yet, can such advertisements tell us something about human nature? Do they make more sense if we look at them in light of evolutionary theory? What, for instance, do men typically want in a wife, and what do most women want in a husband?

This tentacle of scientific inquiry has been driven by an idea that is as simple as it is powerful: the theory of natural selection developed in the mid-nineteenth century by Charles Darwin and Alfred Russell Wallace. Ever since they described the basic mechanism behind directed evolutionary change, no other theory has been able to challenge its ability to use simple ideas to explain a vast range of things about living things, including the origins of not only our own but of all species. The essential core of the theory consists of just two things: variation and selection. Organisms vary in ways that can be passed on to their offspring and also influence their ability to reproduce. Those that reproduce more leave more descendants, so, over time, organisms change. As Darwin recognized when he wrote *The Origin of Species*, this is perhaps easiest to understand by thinking about what it is that people do when they breed animals and plants. Darwin used pigeon breeding as his example in the first chapter of his book, but, perhaps because I have spent so much time with the Mukogodo and their goat herds, I will use goats instead. A goat breeder is faced with a group of individuals that vary in some particular way. Let's say he wants to make them better milk producers. To do this, he simply allows those goats that are the best milk producers to reproduce more than those that are poorer producers. If variations in milk production can indeed be inherited, if there is enough variability to start with, and if the breeder wields a heavy enough hand in determining which goats reproduce and which do not, big changes can be quickly produced. No doubt the Mukogodo and other farmers have understood this process for millennia, but Darwin's insight was that nature does essentially the same thing. It creates problems for organisms to solve and rewards with greater reproduction those varieties that solve them better. Darwin called this "natural selection" in contrast to the "artificial selection" imposed by human breeders. In a nutshell, the name of the game of natural selection can be summed up in the phrase "differential reproduction": Variations that contribute to reproduction persist and spread, those that do not, do not. And as a result of differential reproduction, organisms change, little by little.

Evolution's Groupies

At this point, the application of evolutionary theory to behavior hit a stumbling block that was not decisively overcome until more than a century after

Darwin published his thesis. If natural selection is driven by differential survival and reproduction, does this mean the differential survival and reproduction of individual organisms, groups of organisms, entire species, or what? For some traits, including many physical ones, this is not a crucial issue. Presumably human bipedalism is a good thing for all concerned—individual humans, groups of humans, and the entire human species. But an understanding of the level at which selection acts most strongly can cause drastic changes in how we understand behavior. Depending on whether the forces of selection act most powerfully on one level or another, the process could favor wildly different behavioral traits. If, for example, it is more important for the long-term survival of an organism's genes for the group in which it belongs to survive than for it to survive and reproduce itself, then we would expect organisms to routinely behave in ways that help their groups to survive and spread at the expense of their own ability to survive and reproduce. This was precisely the interpretation given to many animal and human behaviors by researchers in the early 1960s, led by an animal behaviorist named V. C. Wynne-Edwards.[3]

Any individual multicelled organism is really a group, billions of cells working in amazing harmony with a highly developed division of labor. Most of the cells in this group are essentially obligated to be self-sacrificing altruists because they can never reproduce independently. Their reproductive chances (or, more accurately, the reproductive chances of the genes inside them) are entirely wrapped up in those of the whole organism. The self-sacrifice of all of the cells that have no chance of reproducing makes good sense for the genes they share with reproductive cells. Wynne-Edwards argued that this same sort of reasoning could be applied to a higher level, that of an entire population of organisms. Like the cells in a body, individual organisms are also known sometimes to sacrifice their well being and even their lives for the good of the group to which they belong. It is quite common, for instance, for an individual animal to give an alarm call to warn others of a predator even though the call may attract the attention of the predator and make it more likely that the caller will become the predator's main target. Even behaviors like bird flocking made sense to Wynne-Edwards in the light of group selectionist theory as an "epideictic display," letting individual animals get an idea of local population densities so that they can have more or fewer offspring accordingly, taking care not to overrun the local environment's food supply.

This idea was the inspiration for one of the first concerted attempts by anthropologists to apply evolutionary biological theory to human behavior. In the early 1960s, a group of researchers trained largely at Columbia University developed a new, ecologically focused approach to human behavior and culture by combining elements of older anthropological theories with elements, like Wynne-Edwards' theory of group selection, borrowed from ecology, evolutionary biology, and animal-behavior studies. These researchers were, in a sense, the first human sociobiologists because they were the first to apply evolutionary biological theory to the study of human social behavior. An idea that was already commonplace among anthropologists was that one way to understand a society was to understand the "functions" of its various "structures" in much the same way that an anatomist understands an organism by finding how the liver, kidneys, heart, lungs, and so on help keep the organism alive. This analogy meshed easily with the kind of thinking behind Wynne-Edwards' group selectionism and with the newly popular concept of an "ecosystem," and the researchers became known as "neofunctionalists" in contrast to the old-style functionalists whose thinking lacked an evolutionary biological foundation.[4] In light of these theories, the world seemed to be full of societies that had evolved in concert with their ecosystems to maintain an ecologically balanced, stable, and sustainable way of life. Perhaps the most daring of the neofunctionalists' attempts to interpret human behavior was the late University of Michigan anthropologist Roy Rappaport's analysis of a cycle of warfare, feasting, and rituals among a small group of people in New Guinea known as the Tsembaga Maring.[5] Rappaport argued that the Tsembaga's *kaiko* ritual cycle, in which episodes of warfare with neighboring tribes were punctuated with periods of peace and ceremonial feasts that served to thank the Tsembaga's living allies and their helpful ancestors, functioned to maintain a delicate balance between the human population of the Tsembaga, the local pig population, and the carrying capacity of the local environment. Without the cycle, Rappaport argued, the population—particularly that of pigs—would have run amok, outstripping the local food supply and creating an ecological disaster. In other words, the way the ritual cycle works is similar to the way a thermostat in a house works, turning on the furnace when temperatures get too low and the air conditioner when they get too high. According to Wynne-Edwards and his followers the neofunctionalists, such "homeostatic population regulation mechanisms" are nearly ubiquitous. Rappaport was so enthusiastic about this kind of thinking that he even went so far as to interpret the large groups that gather at the ritual feasts to be "epideictic displays" analogous to bird flocks, imparting "to the participants information concerning the population's size or density prior to behavior that may affect that size or density,"[6] not unlike such similar behaviors as the "dancing of gnats and midges, the milling of whirligig-beetles, the manoeuvres of birds and bats at roosting time, the choruses of birds, bats, frogs, insects and shrimps."[7] This no-holds-barred style of drawing analogies between animal behaviors and human cultural systems now seems quite ironic in light of the concern Rappaport expressed late in his life that evolutionary approaches to human behavior may not "give humanity's distinctiveness its due."[8]

Mousehunt

This ambitious and impressive group selectionist edifice began to crumble not long after it was built. The wrecking ball was, more than any other work, a terse, tightly argued little book by George Williams of the State University of New York at Stony Brook titled *Adaptation and Natural Selection*,[9] published two years before Rappaport's book on the Tsembaga. Like the theory of natural selection itself, Williams' argument against Wynne-Edwards' group selectionism was simple and elegant. Let's say we start out with several populations of mice on islands, and let's begin by assuming that group selection has already occurred and that it has provided each population with some mechanism leading individual mice to suppress their own reproduction so that the whole population will not overrun its food supply. If on a particular island a mutant mouse appears that will not go along with this arrangement, reproducing as much as it possibly can instead of holding back for the benefit of the group, then Wynne-Edwards and the group selectionists would concede that on that particular island its descendants would outreproduce and thus outcompete with the mice who continued to suppress their own reproduction. However, to the group selectionists, such reproductively maximizing mice would be as cancer cells in a body, dooming the whole population to extinction. And that is what is meant by "selection on the level of the group": Survival and failure to survive occurring most powerfully not on the level of individual organisms, but on the level of entire groups of organisms.

If that is where the story ends, then we do indeed have group selection. But what if, before that original population infected by the mutant maximizing mice overruns its food supply and dies out, one or more of the mutants get to another population? Then the whole process will repeat itself there. And what if those mutants get to another island before being wiped out again? Well, you get the picture. For group selection to be more powerful than selection on the level of the individual, it has to be difficult for individuals to get from one group to another, and the idea that a whole group of organisms might be wiped out needs to be a real and immediate threat. In nature, these circumstances just do not often happen. In short, group selection is indeed possible, but the circumstances it needs to work—a low rate of migration between populations and a high rate of extinction of entire populations—are so rare as to make group selection itself a rarity in nature.[10]

While very few groups of organisms in nature have the characteristics Williams identified as necessary for group selection to occur, individual organisms have them in spades: It is indeed rare that genes get from one organism to another, the only common way for this to occur being the act of reproduction. And the threat of extinction of entire organisms—also known simply as death—is a real possibility, and indeed an inevitability for every organism so far documented. The only thing that lives on forever are the genes through reproduction. This kind of thinking has led evolutionary biologists since Williams to focus their explanations of behavior on how they could have been produced by selection on individuals' abilities to get copies of their genes into future generations.

People Who Make People

Humans, of course, get copies of their genes into future generations by making more humans. We call these new humans children, and we call this behavior reproduction. Much of the work during the past twenty years or so on the evolutionary biology of human behavior has focused on reproduction, and much of that has been on the details of human mating patterns. What, for instance, are people looking for in mates? Since males and females reproduce somewhat differently, it follows that they ought to go about the business of mating somewhat differently. What makes a male a male and a female a female, after all, regardless of whether one is talking about a human, a grasshopper, or an elm? Certainly a lot of things tend to be different between the sexes, but there are some species, like a lot of birds, that are notoriously difficult to identify as male and female based only on outward appearances. To find out who is a male and who is a female, you have to look at the sex cells, or gametes. The one that produces a relatively small number of relatively large, relatively immobile, and relatively expensive sex cells is the female, and we call those cells eggs. The one that produces a relatively large number of relatively small, relatively mobile, and relatively cheap sex cells is the male, and we call those cells sperm. Since eggs don't move much and are relatively rare and sperm are mobile and abundant, eggs are almost always in short supply from the point of view of sperm. A female usually does not get much benefit from mating with many, many different males. A male, on the other hand, because he can produce lots of sperm in short order, can benefit reproductively from mating with lots of females. The result of this is the dichotomy we see in so many species between the choosy female and the eager, aggressive, easily aroused male that will mate (sometimes not pausing to make sure the object of his desire is even of the correct species) after only the slightest stimulus.

Of course, that picture is a caricature of reality, but it is one that really is approximated by many species. Elephant seals are a classic example.[11] Male elephant seals are loud and aggressive, engaging in bloody fights with each other for control over stretches of the California coastline. The beaches are so valuable to them because that's where they find the females, who need the land to bear and raise their pups. A successful elephant seal male may end up mating with as many as one hundred or more females. A successful female, on the other hand, is not one that scores lots of matings, because she can get all the sperm she needs from a single male. Rather, a female does best by focusing mainly on successfully rearing her pups. It is easy to see how natural selection would act differently on the two sexes, and just looking at elephant seals is enough to see that it has: Male elephant seals are huge beasts with the fatty, bulbous snouts that give them their name, while female elephant seals are only a fraction the weight and just over half the length of the males. This elephant seal pattern is an extremely common one in nature. Males generally tend to focus their attention on doing whatever it takes to get females, be it strutting their stuff for females to admire, battling other males, or holding and defending a nesting site or feeding territory. Females generally have little trouble finding enough sperm to do the job and can benefit most by concentrating on protecting their offspring and obtaining the resources, like food, needed for the young to survive.

Among many species, of course, the differences between the sexes are much less extreme than those seen in elephant seals, with males and females much more similar to each other in behavior and outward appearance. Humans are a good example. Human males tend to be somewhat taller and heavier than females, but not very much. When it comes to behavior, on the other hand, although it is still controversial to say so, a great deal of evidence has accumulated over recent years that supports the idea that human males and females do indeed diverge in significant ways. Consider, for example, sexual fantasies. Donald Symons of the University of California at Santa Barbara and his former student Bruce Ellis make the intriguing argument that it is in people's fantasies that we might get the most insight into underlying desires and predilections because it is in their fantasies that people are allowed to let their imaginations run free, unfettered by the limitations of the real world.[12] To explore this, Symons and Ellis asked a sample of college students about their fantasies. Males reported that they, on average, have sexual fantasies more often than once a day, while females reported that they fantasized, on average, less than once a day. Not a huge difference, but one in the direction expected by evolutionary theory. Since males stand to gain more than females from chance opportunities for sex, they tend to be easier to arouse than females, with the topic of sex frequently bubbling up into their conscious mind. Male fantasies tend to be faster-moving than those of females, with the action quickly moving to the sex act itself, while females tend to take their time in their fantasies before getting to anything explicitly sexual. Males are much more likely than females to fantasize about someone they do not even know or who may simply be a figment of their imaginations, and males are more likely to switch from partner to partner in the middle of a fantasy.

When we move a little closer to reality, we can see some more details about the differences between the sexes. It becomes particularly clear that while males tend to focus on their partners' physical characteristics, females care much more about their partners' and potential partners' ability to control resources and to make commitments to relationships. Several different studies have shown that when men and women are asked to consider various people as potential friends, dates, sex partners, and spouses, variations in status—from, say, a Burger King employee to an architect—have a much greater effect on the men's attractiveness to women than on women's attractiveness to men. Variations in physical attractiveness of these fantasy mates, on the other hand, have a greater effect on women's attractiveness to men than on men's attractiveness to women.[13] As comedian Carol Liefer has explained it, a man becomes turned on by the sight of a naked woman sprawled over the hood of a Porsche, while a woman is turned on by the sight of a fully clothed man sitting behind the wheel of a Porsche.

Let's return to the "personals" or "lonely hearts" advertisements that led off this chapter. Several studies have looked at what such ads reflect about men, women, their mate preferences, and their reproductive strategies.[14] What they have found is that the men who place these ads tend to offer characteristics that correlate with control over resources, such as being resourceful and career oriented. Males tend to seek characteristics in their mates that may, at least among our ancestors, have correlated with fertility, such as having a good figure, youth, sex appeal, and general attractiveness. Females have complementary strategies when they place ads, tending to seek a man who at least has the potential to control significant resources and tending to offer physical attractiveness. In case you are thinking of placing such an ad, words and phrases that are attractive to females include "loving," "reliable," "monogamous," and "career oriented," words and phrases that are attractive to males include "good figure," "attractive," "sexy," "good-looking," and "young," and words and phrases that attract neither sex include "frugal," "lonely," "married," and "like fishing."

The standard social science reaction to this sort of study is that such findings make sense coming from Americans, but what about people in other societies? Indeed, as an anthropologist this is a question that I often ask. Until we test these sorts of hypotheses in a wide variety of societies, we have a hard time making a case that the findings tell us something about a common, evolved human nature and not about the peculiarities of our own culture. Psychologist David Buss of the University of Texas has risen to this challenge by conducting, with the help of colleagues all over the world, a survey of mate preferences in 37 different societies ranging from Americans to Zulu to Chinese.[15] The results are astonishingly consistent across all cultures. First, there is a great deal of overlap between what men and women around the world are looking for in mates, something that is often lost sight of in the quest for sex differences. Men and women everywhere are looking for mates who are kind, understanding, intelligent, healthy, and who have exciting personalities. Nobody deliberately looks for mean, stupid, intolerant, boring people, although, of course, that is what some of us end up with. But there are also some revealing and consistent sex differences in Buss' data, differences that are quite consonant with evolutionary theory's predictions. Males across cultures emphasize more than females the relative youth of their mates and their physical attractiveness. The degree to which males emphasize these characteristics varies from society to society, with Bulgarian men putting the most emphasis on it and Zulu men the least, but the magnitude of the sex difference in emphasis on these characteristics is constant. Females across cultures emphasize more than males the ambition and industriousness of their mates. The only clear exception to these patterns, one that demonstrates that even such things as central to reproduction as mate preferences can be influenced by local circumstances, are the Zulu, a society in which women traditionally did a lot of the most productive farm work and where the men place some importance on their prospective wives' willingness to work.

Anthropologists, like me, are the toughest to sell on the idea that these preferences are present across cultures because they routinely work in societies that are so culturally different from our own. For them, it is not enough to show that urban, literate people—the sort able to answer a survey like Buss'—share particular mating preferences. It also must be shown that people in the exotic, relatively isolated groups that we study also have such tastes. The Kipsigis, a Kenyan group of farmers and herders we met in Chapter 2, qualify. Findings on what Kipsigis men are looking for in their brides and on what the brides and their families are looking for in husbands make sense in light of evolutionary theory.[16] Kipsigis men, like many other men in Africa and elsewhere, must give property, usually including livestock, household goods such as blankets, and sometimes cash, to their in-laws to marry, a payment known as bridewealth. Assuming that Kipsigis men will pay more for women who are the most attractive in their eyes, then variations in Kipsigis bridewealth payments are a good window on the mate preferences of Kipsigis men. One factor that stands out as important is the bride's reproductive potential, and one good indicator of that potential is the bride's age. Girls who have their first menses when they are younger, say 12 or 13, have more children over their lifetimes than girls who do not have their first menses until they are, say, 16, 17, or 18, and those early maturing girls attract significantly higher bridewealth payments than late maturing girls. Girls are choosy in their own way, tending to choose men who control the most resources, even when that means becoming a man's second, third, or fourth wife. To be sure, these things only scratch the surface of a complex issue, and undoubtedly many things other than a bride's reproductive potential and a groom's resources go into Kipsigis' decisions about whom to marry.

Alarming Nepotism

From an individual's point of view, reproduction means making more individuals, and the obvious way to do this is, of course, to mate and produce offspring who will themselves survive and reproduce. Yet, from a gene's point of view, reproduction means getting copies of yourself in future generations, and there is another way to do this besides direct reproduction. Other individuals besides yourself, after all, contain copies of your genes. Your full sibling has, on average, copies of half of your genes by virtue of the fact that you share common ancestors (your mother and father), a half sibling has copies of an average of one quarter of your genes, a cousin has one eighth, and so on. It follows that another way for a gene to get copies of itself into future generations is to get its host individual to help its close relatives. Darwin recognized this as a good explanation for the existence of sterile castes among social insects such as ants, bees, and termites, which help their siblings to reproduce but do not reproduce themselves, and he described it as selection "applied to the family." It was not until 1964, however, that the idea was formalized by W. D. Hamilton, an evolutionary theorist from Oxford.[17] Hamilton noted that it is a simple thing to estimate how many genes individuals share by common descent. This is done with something called the coefficient of relatedness, which was originally developed to determine the likelihood that two related individuals might have the same gene for a heritable disease. The coefficient of relatedness, usually abbreviated by a little "r," is easy to calculate in species like ours that are sexually reproducing and which are "diploid," meaning that we have two sets of our genes, one from our mother and one from our father. Hence, "r" between anyone and his or her parent or child is always one half. For full siblings who are not also identical twins, it is also one half, on average, because they get overlapping sets of genes from the same mother and father. The coefficient of relatedness is reduced by one-half with any generational leap, so that an individual shares one quarter of his genes with his grandmother or niece, half as much as he shares with his mother or full sister. Using this same logic, one is related to one's first cousins by one eighth, to their children by one sixteenth, and so on.

What has become known as "Hamilton's Rule" states that an individual should be altruistic when the cost to itself of the altruistic act, measured in terms of lost future reproduction, are less than the benefits to the recipient of the act, again measured in terms of future reproduction, with the recipient's benefits devalued by the degree to which the two individuals share genes by common descent. For example, should you help your full brother to have six more children by helping him to pay the bridewealth necessary for another wife if by doing so you will be able to afford one less child? Given that you and your brother share, on average, half of your genes, helping him to have six more children is like having three more children (that is, three more copies of your genes) yourself. Because three (the benefit to the recipient devalued by the coefficient of relatedness) is greater than one (the cost to yourself), you should help him. I like to call this "indirect reproduction" to contrast it with direct reproduction, but more common names are kin selection, kin altruism, inclusive-fitness theory, and simply nepotism.

Hamilton's idea has been one of the most important in the development of the new evolutionary biological approach to behavior. In the study of animal behavior, it has shed light not only on the evolution of the social insects, where many individuals are incapable of reproducing directly and instead help their siblings to reproduce, but on altruism and cooperation in a variety of species as well. One now classic study was conducted on alarm calling among Belding's ground squirrels.[18] Because those squirrels that give alarm calls are more likely to be the victims of the predators they are warning about, alarm calling is indeed an altruistic thing for them to do. However, it turns out that not all squirrels do it. Those most likely to give alarm calls are older females. Younger females do it somewhat less often, and males of any age hardly ever. This makes sense once you realize that female squirrels stay in the vicinity of their birth throughout their life, while the males disperse, seeking out mates in other places. As a result, a female squirrel is usually related to a lot of squirrels around her, all of whom stand to benefit from being warned about a predator, while a male may be related to none of the squirrels around him when he spots a predator. That the older females call the most is also significant. The older ones have less future reproduction to lose if they happen to be eaten. In the jargon of the field, their *reproductive value* is lower. Nepotism has also been demonstrated among a variety of bird species, including the African white-fronted bee-eater.[19] Bee-eaters nest in colonies and help feed one another's young. However, they do so not indiscriminately, but rather with a keen eye toward relatedness. In short, the closer the relationship between a helper and a nest owner, the more likely the helper will assist. In many other species, altruism toward kin helps in mating rather than in parenting. Male lions, for example, form coalitions to fight off other males and gain access to prides of females. If the prize of sexual access to the female lions were then distributed evenly among the males of the winning coalition, their ability to form coalitions would not be surprising. Except that the sexual booty is not equally shared, especially not if the group is a relatively large one of four, five, or six males instead of a small one of two or three. Instead, the highest ranking males get several times as many copulations as the lowest ranking males. The key to this seems to be the relatedness among the males. DNA fingerprinting analysis shows that, particularly in the larger groups where some males are acting almost entirely as helpers and getting very few chances to copulate, the males are close relatives such as brothers, half-brothers, and cousins.[20]

Human examples of this nepotistic tendency to favor kin over non-kin and close kin over more distant kin are not hard to find, either. Indeed, this sort of behavior is so widespread that governments and other organizations (i.e., schools, companies, and so on) routinely have rules barring nepotism for fear that people may choose to favor their kin at the expense of their employer's best interests. One dramatic example of people's nepotistic tendencies was serendipitously recorded in the early 1970s when a film crew happened to be visiting a Yanomamö Indian village in Venezuela. Tensions in the village caused by a group of visitors who had overstayed their welcome came to a head one day, and a fight broke out in the village. At first the fight involved only a few individuals, but the conflict quickly spread and escalated from unarmed conflict and shouted insults to long clubs and finally to axes and machetes. Although no one was killed or even cut during the fight, one man was hit on the chest with the blunt side of an ax and knocked unconscious before tensions eased. Thanks to it being filmed, it was possible to piece together exactly which individuals were on which side of the fight. It turns out that it was not simply the visitors versus the locals or one lineage versus another, but one group of males who were closely related among themselves but only distantly related to their enemies battling it out against another group of males who were also closely related among themselves. As we would expect from Hamilton's rule, when push comes to shove, shove comes to club, and club comes to chop, the Yanomamö choose sides with an eye toward helping and being helped by their closest kin.[21]

Researchers have also found a wealth of evidence of people's nepotistic tendencies in a most unlikely place: homicide statistics. Consider, for example, data from Detroit in 1972 on the relationships between murder victims and murderers age 14 (the age at which people start to kill each other in significant numbers) and older when the two were living together at the time of the crime (making the opportunity to kill the same in all cases). In that sample, a person was five to twenty times more likely to be killed by a co-resident spouse or other nonrelative than by a genetic kinsman like a child, parent, or sibling. This pattern repeats itself throughout history and across cultures, people being much more likely to kill nonrelatives than relatives and, on the other hand, to team up preferentially with relatives rather than with nonrelatives to help them with their killing. A murderer in thirteenth-century England, for example, was more than six times as likely to have a kinsman as a co-offender than he was to kill a kinsman.[22]

Unfortunately for world peace, this nepotistic tendency does not extend far beyond immediate family members. This is because *r*, the coefficient of relatedness, diminishes quickly with the distance of genetic relationships. Brothers and sisters may share an average of half their genes by common descent, but first cousins share only an eighth, second cousins only one thirty-second, third cousins only one one hundred and twenty-eighth, and so on. Bosnians and Serbians or North and South Koreans may seem to be closely related, sharing as they do common culture and language, but *r* between any two randomly chosen individuals on either side of those conflicts is likely to be a vanishingly small fraction.

A Fractious Topic

When this biological—indeed, *genetic*—approach to human kinship was first introduced in the late 1970s, it ran straight up against the previous several decades of opinion in all of the social and behavioral sciences, but it was especially disturbing to anthropologists. For many of them, all of this talk about kinship was just too much. Kinship, after all, was *the* classic subject of their field, what they studied better and more thoroughly than anyone else, and they *knew* that biology was irrelevant to understanding it. As anthropology's leading critic of sociobiology, the University of Chicago's Marshall Sahlins, put it at the time, "the issue between sociobiology and social anthropology is decisively joined on the field of kinship."[23] Some of Sahlins' arguments against the idea of indirect reproduction were, frankly, laughable. He argued, for instance, that neither animals nor most humans could possibly behave according to the calculus of genetic relatedness because they cannot possibly calculate fractions. This has been compared to arguing that baseball players should not be able to catch balls because they cannot solve in their heads the differential equations needed to describe the trajectory of a flying object. Sahlins did, however, make one clear-cut, falsifiable, and therefore potentially testable prediction: "There is not a single system of marriage, postmarital residence, family organization, interpersonal kinship, or common descent in human societies that does not set up a different calculus of relationship and social action than is indicated by the principles of kin selection."[24] In other words, he argued, in no society on Earth do people behave in accordance with the predictions of selfish gene theory. Behavior is instead determined by the arbitrary, capricious, and infinitely variable dictates of culture.

A few anthropologists took this prediction seriously and set out to test it. One was Kristen Hawkes, who at the time had recently received her doctorate from the University of Washington for research among the Binumarien, an egalitarian tribal people who raise pigs and sweet potatoes in the highlands of New Guinea. She was trained as a traditional cultural anthropologist, and she fully expected to be able to use her data on Binumarien kinship and behavior to prove Sahlins right and selfish gene theory wrong. It didn't turn out that way. Sahlins was right, of course, that the terms the Binumarien use for their kin do not correspond exactly with genetic relatedness. This is true in virtually all languages. In English, for example, your "uncle" may be your parent's brother and hence share an average of one quarter of his genome with you, or he might be your parent's sister's husband and hence share no genes with you at all. For example, men who in our terminology would be called "cousins" are instead referred to as "brothers." But, Hawkes found to her surprise, this did not mean that the Binumarien don't do what selfish gene theory would predict them to do. In fact, she found that when it comes to helping one another, the Binumarien behave just as selfish gene theory would predict, helping genetically close kin more than genetically distant kin, regardless of the kin terms used. Biological siblings are more likely to help one another than biological cousins, despite the fact that they are referred to by the same kin term.[25]

The effects these findings had on Hawkes was dramatic. She rapidly developed an appreciation and detailed understanding of evolutionary theory and how it applies to behavior, going on to become one of anthropology's most important theoreticians. Most recently, she has forced a complete reconsideration of the origins of the custom of marriage. She also has tested her ideas using data from new fieldwork, conducting detailed studies of three other societies besides the Binumarien.[26]

The Utility of It All

Hawkes' personal transformation mirrors that of a significant proportion of other anthropologists. Since the late 1970s, a wide range of classic anthropological topics, including not only kinship but also marriage customs such as bridewealth and dowry, foraging techniques, the ways that food and other goods are distributed in small-scale societies, and different ways of parenting, have become clearer, thanks to evolutionary theory, and it is no longer possible for anthropologists to claim to know something about them without being familiar with this body of research. The same is increasingly true in the other social and behavioral sciences. The effect has perhaps been greatest in psychology, where evolutionary ideas are transforming our understanding of cognition, personality, emotions, social interaction, and even mental illness.

The implications for the social sciences of their incorporation into the blob are both less and more than one might imagine. On the one hand, much of what social scientists have done will and should continue much as it has before. Economists, for example, have developed an impressive body of formal theory successfully explaining a wide variety of phenomenon, from the way money flows through an economy to the behaviors of institutions like business firms and the Federal Reserve Bank. There is no need nor reason to conduct, say, a study of Alan Greenspan's reproductive success to better understand the behavior of the Fed. The situation is similar in other social sciences. Linking them with the rest of the sciences through an understanding of the biology of human behavior would still leave intact virtually all that they have accomplished. I do not, for example, foresee the transformation of political science by any new biologically based models of the strategies used by lobbyists.

On the other hand, linking the study of society to the rest of the sciences will have some real benefits for those fields. In economics, for example, insights from evolutionary biology can help flesh out the concept of "utility." Economists are able to develop their elaborate formal theoretical models in part because they begin with the simplifying assumption that people strive to maximize their utility. What, exactly, "utility" may be for a given person is usually set aside as a question properly answered by non-economists. Evolutionary theory can help by making testable predictions about precisely what people in various situations ought to be striving for given our species' history of natural selection. This might be especially helpful in demography, a sort of hybrid social science in which many of the dominant models are essentially economic ones, and people's reproductive choices—how many children to have, when to have them, which sex of offspring to favor, and so on—are examined in terms of their effect on utility. Often, demographers treat "utility" simply as material wealth, and so children are seen not as ends in and of themselves but as producers and consumers. And, indeed, children do produce and consume, and so anyone who cares about people's reproductive decisions should care about how productive children are in various situations and how much they consume. But to most demographers, the fundamental issue of why people have children at all, especially in situations where they consume far more than they produce, is a mystery. Of course, from the point of view of evolutionary biology, this is no problem at all.

Another way to understand the basic complementarity—rather than conflict—of biological and existing approaches to behavior and society is to realize that virtually any phenomenon can be correctly and accurately attributed to a variety of causes. One way different causes might fit together is "vertically," with some being close in time and space to the phenomenon in question and others farther away. This idea of "levels of explanation" has long been a mainstay of biological thought.[27] Different sorts of biologists with different interests and different purposes take different, but complementary, views of causation. Take, for instance, the gagging reflex. A doctor interested in treating a patient with a risk of choking on bites of food because of a faulty gagging reflex would be interested in its mechanics, how it is supposed to function in a healthy individual. Biologists call this sort of explanation, typically a mechanistic one that stays close to the phenomenon at hand, "proximate." A developmental biologist, interested in finding out why some people do not end up with healthy gagging reflexes, would take a step back from the mechanics of choking itself and look instead at how the biological structures necessary for choking develop as an organism grows from zygote to adult. This is referred to as a "developmental" or "ontological" explanation. Someone like me, who is interested in how natural selection has affected organisms in their evolutionary pasts, would be interested in reconstructing the selection pressures necessary for producing such a reflex: How much sensitivity to foreign objects in the throat is a good thing that would have helped our ancestors to survive and reproduce and how much would have impeded swallowing and hence have been too much? And, finally, paleontologists (which includes most physical anthropologists) would be interested in the trait's history over long spans of evolutionary time. Such "phylogenetic" explanations are something we came across in Chapter 2 under the label of phylogenetic inertia, the idea that an organism's past is one determinant of its future evolution.

Proximate explanations are becoming a particularly important element in evolutionary studies of behavior. Many researchers, no longer satisfied by explaining precisely how some behavior might be adaptive, want also to explain the details of how the behavior is produced. Take, for instance, the problem of how individual animals know their relatives. Without some clues about this, there is no way for Hamilton's rule to operate. But, as Sahlins pointed out, animals cannot handle fractions and hence cannot calculate the coefficient of relatedness. Animal behaviorists have responded to this challenge with detailed studies of the mechanisms of kin recognition.[28] It turns out that while some organisms use cues like scent to tell relatives from nonrelatives, others use simple clues from their living situations. If, for instance, your litter mates are normally your siblings, then it makes sense to treat them as such.

A nice example of an adaptive human behavior for which we have a good grasp of the proximate mechanisms involved is birth spacing among the !Kung. !Kung women give birth, on average, only every four years, which is not often compared to most women in traditional societies. This birth rate seems to be an optimal one for them because if they were to give birth more often the women would have to work a great deal harder hauling children and gathering food, and their child mortality rates would increase sharply as a result. They maintain this wide birth spacing without any modern contraceptives, relying instead on a degree of sexual abstinence following birth and nursing to reduce the chance that a woman will get pregnant. Nursing does this by stimulating the production of a hormone that suppresses ovulation. This works as a birth-control technique among the !Kung because !Kung women practice on-demand nursing, which keeps their hormonal levels high. Western women, who often put their babies on nursing schedules rather than nursing them on demand, may find their hormonal levels can drop far enough and for long enough periods between bouts of nursing for ovulation to resume not long after birth.[29]

Explanations of a single phenomenon may also fit together "horizontally," meaning that something is caused by a variety of things that are all more or less the same causal distance from it. A car accident, for example, might be caused by a combination of a wet road, a tired driver, bad tires, and an attempt to avoid a pedestrian. If any one element were removed from the scene, then perhaps the accident would never have occurred. And clearly it would be a mistake to try to explain such an accident by focusing on just one element—the bald tires, say—while ignoring or belittling all of the others.

Yet, in a sense, this is what those of us who look at human nature through the eyes of evolutionary theory have been doing for the past twenty years or so: Focusing on a single, albeit extraordinarily important thing that contributes to human behavior, while ignoring other causes, like someone who studies traffic accidents who has become fascinated by the new discovery that sometimes they involve bad brakes. It is high time that we found a way of including in our analysis other influences on behavior, such as culture. We'll wrestle with the problem of how to do that in the next two chapters.

5

An Infectious Idea

Go ye therefore, and teach all nations, baptizing them in the name of the Father, and of the Son, and of the Holy Ghost: Teaching them to observe all things whatsoever I have commanded you.

—statement attributed to Jesus (Matthew 28:19–20)

You must send this on in 1 hour after reading this letter to ten different people. If you do this, you will receive luck in love. The person that you are most attracted to will soon return your feelings. THIS IS NOT A JOKE!!!!!!! You have read the warnings, you must send this on!!!!! Eric Mancough send [sic] this letter out within 45 minutes of reading it. Not even 4 hours later was he walking along the street when he ran into Ann Heartearn, his secret love for 5 years. Ann came up to him and told him of her passionate crush on him that she had had for 2 years. Ann and Eric are still married with five children, happy as ever.

—from an undated chain letter[1]

Just Forget It

In February of 1989 I happened to be watching television when suddenly some familiar-looking people appeared on the screen. I recognized them at once as warriors and girls from the Samburu tribe, a strikingly handsome and proud group of people who live just north of the Mukogodo and who speak a dialect of their same Maasai language. The only odd thing about these particular Samburu was that they were wearing Nike hiking boots. At the end of the brief commercial, one of the warriors turned to the camera and said, "*Mayieu kuna. Injooki inamuka sapukin.*" The advertisers translated this phrase for their American audience as the Nike slogan: "Just do it." The only problem for Nike was that that was not what the young man said. Actually, his statement translates much better as "I don't want these. Give me big shoes." In other words, the ones he had were too small for him, so he was asking for a larger size.

Thanks to my wife, who was a journalist at the time, the story made it onto the front page of *USA Today.* From there it quickly spread into dozens of newspapers and magazines around the world. I was even interviewed on the television program *Entertainment Tonight* and mentioned in Johnny Carson's *Tonight Show* monologue. For three or four days, I was very busy, and I had a lot of fun. Despite the embarrassment, the Nike company appeared to appreciate the tremendous amount of free publicity being generated for their excellent line of hiking boots, and to express their gratitude they sent me a free pair. I wore them during my last visit to the Mukogodo, where, unintentionally bringing the whole thing full circle, I passed them on to a Mukogodo friend (who did not, however, complain about the size).

Cute story, don't you think? Now, please forget it.

Although the attention generated by that story faded after about a week, a couple of years later, it started to come back. For the past few years I have been receiving, on average, about one inquiry a month about that incident back in 1989. The reason for the renewed attention, it seems, is simple: the Internet. The creation of a worldwide network of computers, with tens of millions of users in the United States alone, has created an opportunity for little stories like the Nike commercial to gain a life of their own and to persist and spread long after their newsworthiness has faded. A quick search of the World Wide Web using a typical search engine for my name and the word "Nike" comes back with more than two dozen hits. Most of these are taken from a *Forbes* magazine article about it that ran back in 1989, but the date never appears along with the story, so it never looks old, leaving people free to copy it onto their own web pages and to believe that it happened just yesterday rather than a decade ago.

Teach Your Children Well

That story and the Nike slogan "Just do it" itself are good examples of successful cultural traits, little snippets of information that, for some reason or another, are successfully motivating people to copy them again and again.

They are, in other words, a lot like successful genes, which also are bits of information that, for some reason or another, help their carriers to make copies of themselves. One approach to the problem of how to fit culture into the new evolutionary study of behavior is based on just this analogy: Culture traits are, in many ways, like genes, an alternate system of information transfer over the generations, a medium in which bits of information can take on lives of their own.

People have long had an intuitive understanding of the basic idea here: Some ideas catch on and spread, and may even last a long time in a population, while others fail to win converts and die out. Pop-song writers, advertising agents, and founders of cults are all in search of different types of cultural traits that will be successful in spreading from mind to mind. It was only fairly recently, however, that this idea was formalized and scientifically tested. My former graduate advisor at Northwestern University, William Irons, was one of the first to try to incorporate culture into the developing evolutionary biological approach to behavior described in the last chapter, and he did it using a variant of this basic analogy. He passed it on to me, and now I'm passing it on to you.

Irons came to this approach through a rather roundabout way. Like many anthropologists in the late 1960s, he had been impressed by Roy Rappaport's analysis of the Tsembaga Maring ritual cycle as a way of keeping the numbers of people and domesticated animals in an area in harmony with their ecosystem (see Chapter 4). He set out to use this sort of group selectionist thinking about population regulation mechanisms in a study of the Yomut Turkmen, a Turkic-speaking pastoralist people in northern Iran whom he had studied for his dissertation. As is often the case in science, his choice of research problem was not solely a result of dry, detached reasoning about what sorts of problems are the most urgent in a particular field. Rather, like many other people at a time when environmentalism was becoming popular, he found the idea that people in traditional societies have evolved ways of living in balance with their environments to be aesthetically pleasing. Although he knew enough evolutionary biology to realize that most people in that field did not consider group selection to be important for most species, he agreed with most cultural anthropologists in believing that culture would somehow make our species different in this regard.[2]

Unfortunately for Irons' aesthetic sense, his results did not support the group selectionist hypothesis. Far from regulating their population to keep it in balance with their environment, Irons' data forced him to conclude that the Yomut were, in fact, trying as hard as possible to turn resources into people, for example, to reproduce as much as they could, just as mainstream selfish gene theory would have predicted.

Irons realized, however, that people in their everyday lives do not strive in some simple and straightforward way to reproduce. Rather, they strive for a variety of more real and immediate goals, like getting enough to eat, avoiding disease, amassing wealth, and achieving status. Furthermore, he realized that people's particular goals vary from group to group, with some groups emphasizing the accumulation of wealth while in other societies there is virtually no wealth—no land ownership, no livestock, no precious metals—to accumulate in the first place. This very flexibility, Irons reasoned, might be what makes culture adaptive, and what has helped our species to be successful in the game of reproduction. Just as organisms evolve through natural selection to fit their changing environments, he argued, so may culture evolve to track changing circumstances. As your favorite food becomes less abundant, you become less picky, and you teach your children to do the same. As populations become denser, you start leaving your fields fallow for shorter and shorter periods, cropping them more and more frequently, while spending more time and energy building irrigation systems, composting vegetation and manure, applying fertilizer, and so on, and you teach your children to do the same. In traditional societies much of culture was passed from parents to children, and so on the whole, it was likely to be composed of beneficial advice and information about how best to get along in the world.

That much is not controversial, but Irons took a step not taken by most anthropologists: He was very clear about what he meant by "adaptive." In evolutionary biology, "adaptive" means helping an organism to pass on its genes, helping it win in the game of differential reproduction. If culture is adaptive, then that means being good at whatever your culture tells you is worth doing in life ought to lead to more success in that game. Culturally defined success, whether it is wealth, prestige, humility, fierceness, peacefulness, or whatever, should correlate with reproductive success. As circumstances change and what used to lead to greater reproduction no longer works, people should learn new ways and should pass them on to their children. In short, culture should track whatever it is that helps individuals pass on their genes the way evolving organisms track their environments.[3]

Irons' idea works almost embarrassingly well. So far it has been tested in about two dozen small-scale societies that resemble those in which humans spent most of their evolutionary history, and it is a resounding success in every one. Irons' own study of the Yomut Turkmen is a case in point. The Yomut were traditionally pastoralists, making a living from their herds of sheep and, especially in recent years, some farming. As in many traditional societies, Yomut men were allowed multiple wives. But, also as in many traditional societies, wives did not come cheap. Yomut men had to make substantial bridewealth payments to their in-laws to marry. What does Yomut culture value? The Yomut are unequivocal on this point: A Yomut man's goal is to get rich. According to Irons, then, getting rich (culturally defined success) should lead to enhanced reproduction (biologically defined success). And it does. Richer Yomut men reproduce at a much higher rate than poorer ones. Mostly this is caused by their ability to afford more wives and to support larger numbers of children, but that is not the whole story. Individual women who are married to richer Yomut men also reproduce at a higher rate than those married to poorer ones because they have better nutrition, receive better medical care, and do not perform as much strenuous physical labor. So being richer helps, even if you are not polygynous.

The same result has been found in several similar societies. The Mukogodo, for example, share some basic similarities with the Yomut. They also are pastoralists, allow polygyny, value the accumulation of livestock (though few of them are able to do very well at this), and pay bridewealth. Not surprisingly, richer Mukogodo men have more children than poorer ones. Skeptics have argued that perhaps the reason wealth and reproductive success are linked is not because wealth leads to more children, but because more children lead to wealth. After all, in traditional societies it is quite common for children to spend a lot of their time working. But in the Mukogodo case, at least, this analysis does not work. Even if we look only at Mukogodo men with one wife and children too small to do any productive work, we still find that wealth leads to greater reproductive success. The labor provided by wives and children may help somewhat, but clearly that is not the whole story. Achieving the culturally defined goal of wealth accumulation really does lead to higher reproductive success, just as Irons predicts.[4]

Another angle is to look at societies where something besides wealth is defined as "success." In many traditional societies, there is virtually no "wealth." Everyone has essentially the same material possessions, and there is no point in trying to accumulate anything. What happens in those societies? Among the hunting and gathering Ache of Paraguay, for example, success for men is being a good hunter, and good hunting leads to greater reproductive success. The reason is not because the good hunters have more wives at the same time, because the Ache, like most hunter-gatherers, seldom practice polygyny. The reason, rather, appears to be twofold. First, good hunters have more extramarital affairs than poor hunters and sire more offspring that way.

Since the meat produced by the good hunters is shared by the whole group, the other men have an incentive to tolerate a certain amount of philandering on the part of good hunters. Good Ache hunters are a little like star football players: Other Ache turn a blind eye to their misdemeanors for fear that another team (or another foraging band) may bid them away. Second, the children of good hunters, whether legitimate or not, are treated better by the group than the children of poorer hunters, and as a result they survive better. Again, the community has an incentive to make good hunters happy.[5]

The Yanomamö of Venezuela and Brazil also illustrate the idea that achieving cultural success need not mean accumulating wealth. The Yanomamö are horticulturalists and hunters, subsisting mainly on plantains. They have no livestock or other wealth to accumulate, and all men have virtually the same property. To a Yanomamö, success does not mean being wealthy, it means being fierce and successful in warfare. In particular, special status is given to men, called *unokai*, who have taken part in the killing of other men. In accordance with Irons' hypothesis, men who have *unokai*ed are more successful reproductively than those who have not.[6] This does not, of course, mean that what is true of the Yanomamö is true of everyone else. No one argues that aggressiveness *universally* leads to greater reproduction. Remember, Irons' hypothesis is that culture tracks whatever *locally* enhances reproduction. In the Yanomamö case, having a reputation for ferocity seems to do the trick. Elsewhere, peacefulness and having an even, ecumenical disposition may be more appropriate. Among the nineteenth-century Cheyenne, for example, the most prestigious men were not the "war chiefs," but rather the "peace chiefs."[7]

Clearly, in traditional societies, achieving culturally defined success does routinely lead to enhanced reproductive success. But what about when things change? Does Irons' broader hypothesis that culture tracks whatever enhances reproduction, changing as circumstances change, really work, or does it only work when things are static? So far, my study of the Mukogodo is the only one to really test this. As explained in Chapter 1, the Mukogodo once lived in caves, eating wild animals, honey, and some wild plants. They spoke their own language called Yaaku and paid beehives—simply hollowed logs—as bridewealth. Then, early in this century, things began to change. For reasons that had mainly to do with the new British colonial presence in Kenya, the Mukogodo increasingly came into contact with a variety of Maasai-speaking pastoralist groups, and they started to marry among them. Mostly the trade was one way: Mukogodo women married non-Mukogodo men. Especially at the beginning, few women went the other way. When

Mukogodo men married their daughters off to the pastoralists, they obtained not a bunch of hollowed logs they could have made themselves, but several cattle and often some sheep and goats. Soon, no one was about to let his daughter marry for mere beehives, and to get married, Mukogodo men had to obtain livestock and become pastoralists. Some succeeded by marrying their daughters or sisters off to pastoralists. Some traded elephant tusks and other wildlife trophies. Some got jobs, earned cash, and used it to buy livestock. Many, however, never got livestock, never married, and presumably never reproduced. About a third of all Mukogodo men who entered the marriage market at the peak of the transition to pastoralism in the 1920s and 1930s never married. In a period of only about ten years, from 1925 to 1936, the Mukogodo went from living in caves and living as foragers to being virtually indistinguishable from the Maasai. They even abandoned their old Yaaku language in favor of Maasai, along with their religion and other aspects of their culture. Although it certainly would be nice to have more studies that test this aspect of Irons' idea, this case is clear: Mukogodo culture did a virtual hairpin turn to track the behaviors that tracked fitness in their new social environment.[8]

Off-Track

Our society, of course, does not neatly fit Irons' hypothesis. People in Western, industrialized societies are the wealthiest people the world has ever seen, yet they have some of the lowest rates of reproduction in the world. There may be a variety of reasons for this. Some have suggested that it has to do with the availability of good birth control. Yet, birth rates declined in Western countries long before reliable, modern methods of birth control became available, so this cannot be the whole story. Others have pointed out that the networks of kin that help people in traditional societies to raise their children have largely broken down in our society. While in times past the costs of another child would be spread widely throughout a large, extended family, and another child was a relatively inexpensive decision for a man and woman to make, in our society the costs of another child are typically borne almost entirely by the parents, possibly making them hesitate a bit more before taking that big—and increasingly expensive—step.[9]

To other researchers, the key to the decline in family size in recent times seems to be the way that the traditional link between wealth and the ability to raise children has been severed in modern societies. In traditional societies, an additional child costs a poor man and a rich man about the same.

Rich people have more resources than poor people, so they tend to be able to afford more children. However, in societies such as ours, where people have a wide range of choices about which clothes to buy for their children, which schools to send them to, and so on, how one treats one's children has itself become an indicator of status. A rich couple wanting to maintain or enhance its status cannot simply use its vast resources to have lots of poorly clothed, fed, medicated, and educated children. To do so would be disastrous for the couple's status. Instead, they may choose to have a smaller number of very well clothed, fed, medicated, and educated children, reducing their reproductive success but maintaining their status and that of their children. Maintaining status in this way may not make ultimate reproductive sense, but it makes a lot of sense if, as Irons has argued, our minds evolved in societies in which status was routinely rewarded by reproduction.

For greater insight into societies like ours, let us look at the one good, detailed examination of Irons' hypothesis in an industrialized Western setting, conducted a few years ago by Daniel Pérusse of the University of Montreal.[10] Pérusse surveyed several hundred French Canadian men to find out the relationship between their marital status, sexual behavior, and socioeconomic status. What he found was that, underneath it all, Irons' hypothesis still is not so far off. While actual reproductive success was not enhanced by men's socioeconomic status, men's access to opportunities to conceive children was much improved by high status. Men with lots of income and with prestigious jobs had significantly more sexual encounters with significantly more women than men with lower incomes and less prestigious jobs. What keeps the actual reproductive rates of higher- and lower-status men more or less equal is two things. First, monogamy really does put a damper on men's sexual lives. Some married men did report considerable numbers of extramarital affairs, but for the most part having only one steady partner made poor and rich married men more or less equal in terms of their access to opportunities to conceive. Most of the difference between the mating success of higher- and lower-status men occurs among those who are not married. Second, birth control is important. Many more "opportunities to conceive" would have led to real conceptions were it not for the pill, condoms, and so on.

So far, so good. Indeed, the great success of this hypothesis has helped to justify the wider project of an evolutionary approach to human affairs. However, this success hides a paradox. Even though Irons' idea has everything to do with culture, the support it has received has also helped to justify the way that folks such as myself have virtually ignored culture. After all, if culture tracks behaviors that enhance reproductive success, then culture is a proximate mechanism for tracking environmental variation and defining what is adaptive in a simple and direct way. If culture is just a strong, reliable, uncomplicated link in a chain between adaptation and behavior, then we can assume that culture will define what is locally adaptive and that people will do what culture tells them to do. If this were the case, we could go on borrowing models from animal behavior studies, assuming that these models will predict behavior without working culture into the picture at all.

The problem is that there are many aspects of culture that clearly do not fit this simple environmental tracking model. Irons' hypothesis does not lead us to think about all of the examples of mismatches between culture and behavior described in Chapter 1. If culture helps people do whatever enhances reproduction given local circumstances, then why isn't culture telling Mukogodo parents to favor their daughters? And why are there so many other examples of culture telling people one thing and people doing another thing entirely? In his original paper on this hypothesis, Irons explicitly limited its application to cultural traits that do influence behavior, excluding "verbal preferences which never affect behavior." Why, then do such verbal preferences exist at all? Clearly, culture is not just a simple and reliable link between adaptation and behavior. Something else is going on, something complex and potentially interesting.

A Parallel Track

Just as Irons was publishing his theory that culture, on the whole, leads people to behave adaptively, another group of researchers was taking the gene-cultural analogy and running with it, but in a slightly different direction. This approach was crystallized and given widespread attention largely as the result of the term "meme," coined by evolutionary biologist Richard Dawkins in his 1976 book *The Selfish Gene*. Because it sounds like "gene," looks like the French word *même*, meaning "same," and shares a Greek root with words like "imitation," "meme" conjures up appropriate images of something that is copied and transmitted from person to person. A meme might, for example, be a popular fashion. You see someone with a particular hair style, and you change yours to match. Others see how good you look with your new hair, and they change theirs, and so on. As I write this, a large and growing proportion of female students in my classes are sporting a new hairstyle in imitation of a character in a television program. The idea of the meme is itself a meme, and a successful one at that, having been the subject of a recent spate of popular books.[11]

Some memes are, like genes, passed from parents to their children in what cultural transmission theorists refer to as "vertical transmission." The sorts of cultural values Irons' hypothesis focuses on, for example, are mostly embodied as examples, advice, and expectations passed from parents to their children. Just as genes only remain in a gene pool if they help their bearers to reproduce, vertically transmitted cultural traits will only continue to be passed from parent to child if they help parents to have children, and the more they help, the more widespread they become. As a result, the correspondence between cultural values and reproductive success that Irons predicted and subsequently found makes good sense: Just as those genes spread that help their bearers to have more offspring, so should those vertically transmitted memes spread that help their bearers to have more offspring.

Culture traits can also be passed the way viruses are, *horizontally* from one individual to some unrelated individual. Unlike vertically transmitted traits, cultural traits that successfully spread horizontally into many different human heads may have no good and possibly even some very bad effects on the owners of those heads. Religious beliefs are good candidates for this viral analogy. Someone convinces you of a particular belief, you pass it on to someone else, and so on. So much the better for this virus of a meme if passing it on to others is portrayed as an essential part of believing it yourself. Thus do proselytizing religions (and chain letters) spread around the globe.[12]

When the idea of memetics (as this approach is now popularly called) was first proposed, it was seen by many as an alternative, even a rival, to the idea of studying the influences of our species' biological evolutionary heritage on our behavior. Richard Dawkins, for example, argued that the evolutionary biological study of human behavior "did not begin to square up to the formidable challenge of explaining culture, cultural evolution, and the immense differences between human cultures around the world. . . . I think we have got to start again and go right back to first principles."[13] As a result of this sort of either/or rhetoric, two camps emerged, one that focused on traditional behavioral ecology, borrowing models from animal behavior studies (models that do not include culture) and applying them to humans, and another that busied itself with creating new models of the transmission and evolution of cultural traits.

That situation was reminiscent in many ways of a split in biological circles early in this century. Although Gregor Mendel is rightly given credit in textbooks for discovering the rules of genetic inheritance, it was not until those rules were rediscovered around the turn of the century—thirty-five years after Mendel—that they became widely known among biologists. That event

exacerbated an already existing split within biology over the relative importance of the mechanisms of inheritance, on the one hand, and the process of
natural selection, on the other, to the evolution of species. Extremists on the
genetics side held that the new discoveries of the rules of inheritance and of
the existence of genetic mutations eliminated the need for Darwin's theory
entirely. It was not until the 1930s and 1940s that evolutionary biologists developed an approach that saw these two phenomena as complementary parts
of a single process, a development known as the "modern synthesis" or "neo-
Darwinism."

Similarly, the past couple of decades have seen the development of an appreciation of the value of the other position on both sides of the split in the
evolutionary study of human behavior. This reconciliation has come about
largely as a result of a great deal of real-world research with solid, interesting,
and often surprising findings. The basics of the non-cultural evolutionary biology of human behavior were covered in Chapter 4. Suffice it to say that after two decades of research it is no longer easy for anyone to maintain the belief that evolutionary biology is irrelevant to an understanding of human
behavior.

The memeticists have been busy, too, and they have come up with some
good examples of how cultures and genes have evolved together. Sometimes
this means that they help one another, as in Irons' hypothesis that the cultural values people teach their children will, by and large, lead to greater reproduction. But, of course, culture also has the potential to lead people to do
things that are maladaptive but that help the cultural traits themselves to
spread. One good example of a cultural trait that spread quickly through a
group despite its bad consequences for individuals who carried it is the practice of cannibalism among the Fore of Papua New Guinea.[14] The Fore had a
long-standing tradition of funerary feasts, which at one time involved consumption of pork but not human flesh. Cannibalism was added to the custom relatively recently, spreading through various subgroups of the Fore during the past century or so. The new cannibalism involved eating dead
members of one's own group, which is called "endocannibalism," rather than
dead enemies, which is called "exocannibalism." Some Fore were struck by
how sensible and enjoyable endocannibalism was. One was quoted as saying,
"This is sweet. What is the matter with us, are we mad? Here is good food
and we have neglected to eat it. In [the] future we shall always eat the dead,
men, women, and children. Why should we throw away good meat? It is not
right!" Many Fore remarked that human flesh reminded them of their favorite meat, pork, and that the best meat was to be had from those who had

died quickly rather than those who wasted away, because they had more fat. They even developed customs regarding which relatives of the dead person had the right to eat particular body parts. For example, a man's wife got to eat the flesh around her dead husband's pelvic bone and spine, while a man's sister got to eat her brother's brain. This continued until the 1950s, when the central government ended the practice.

By itself, Fore endocannibalism may strike us as strange and even repugnant, but it is not obviously maladaptive. It may even have helped some Fore to live healthier, longer, and happier lives because of the addition of needed proteins and fats to their diets. But, unbeknownst to the Fore, a real biological pathogen was being spread along with the culture trait of endocannibalism. The pathogen caused a degenerative and fatal nerve disease known as *kuru*, a Fore word meaning trembling, shivering, fear, and cold. *Kuru* is similar to a sheep disease called scrapie, "mad cow disease" (bovine spongiform encephalopathy) which has caused so much fear recently among British beef eaters, and the human Creutzfeldt-Jakob disease. A number of things pointed to cannibalism as having a key role in the spread of the disease. For example, most of the deaths from *kuru* were among women, who were also the main consumers of human flesh. Fore men avoided it, arguing that consumption of anything other than pork would weaken them and make them less able to defend their communities. Furthermore, deaths from *kuru* tapered off after cannibalism was ended in the 1950s.

As interesting as the Fore cannibalism example is, its very obscurity suggests something about maladaptive cultural traits: They are surprisingly hard to find. Although it may seem logical that culture traits could frequently lead people to do maladaptive things, as a practical matter it is not easy to find examples of traits that are popular among large numbers of people for long periods of time that routinely lead to maladaptive consequences (like premature death or reduced reproduction) unless they are being forced to do it. For instance, the practice of slavery is not very adaptive for the slaves involved, but then it isn't their choice to be slaves in the first place. They are behaving maladaptively only because someone else is forcing them to.

Perhaps, if cultural traits are sometimes like viruses, then, just as we have an immune system to fight off biological viruses, so should we also have one to fight off cultural ones. And we do: It's called the brain. If culture were not, most of the time and in most places throughout human evolution, a good thing, then it would be a strange thing indeed if natural selection were to have favored the evolution of an organ so large, so expensive,[15] and so well designed for dealing with the world created by culture as the human brain.

Certainly culture can lead people to do maladaptive things, and a complete theory of culture should be able to handle those instances, but they ought to be relatively unusual. If they were common, you would not be reading this. Instead, we would be chimps, at best, and our culture would be rudimentary or nonexistent. The brain should act as a sort of mental immune system, examining cultural ideas as they come in, considering their likely consequences, rejecting the ones that are liable to do harm and accepting those that are apt to help. Like our actual immune systems, the brain is not always right, but by now it should have evolved some pretty good rules of thumb.

On those rare occasions when we do find people voluntarily adhering to maladaptive cultural traits, it is usually because the maladaptiveness of the traits is hard for our cultural immune system to discern. The Fore, for example, were keenly aware that something was wrong as so many of them fell victim to *kuru*, but they had no idea that their newfound practice of cannibalism was to blame. Their ignorance is not surprising given that it took Western scientists many years of dedicated work to track down the details of the epidemic, a medical detective story that earned a Nobel prize for the lead researcher, Carleton Gajdusek of the National Institutes of Health. When it is easier to see the connection between a cultural trait and its maladaptive consequences, people usually drop it quickly unless there is some compensating benefit (like enhanced social status) or they are being forced to adhere to it.

Sneaking Groups in the Back Door

The theory of memetics has one implication that may warm the hearts of those who are made uncomfortable by selfish-gene theory. Although the consensus among evolutionary theorists remains that *biological* group selection is unlikely to be a powerful force in evolution, it is possible that *cultural* group selection has been significant in the evolution of our species' behaviors.[16] As we saw in Chapter 4, biological group selection requires that migration between groups be rare and that the extinction of entire groups be a real threat. Otherwise, the forces of selection at the level of the individual and of the gene will easily swamp the effects of group selection. However, cultural group selection could, theoretically at least, occur much more easily. If groups differ in terms of the cultural traits of their members and if those group-level differences lead some groups to be more successful than others, then cultural group selection can be said to have occurred. This does not require either that migration between groups be rare or that anybody—group or individual—die, or even that anybody act altruistically. All it requires is

that group differences be maintained long enough for some groups to pros-
per and grow and others to fade away. Between-group differences can be the
result of people's well-documented tendency to conform to local standards of
behavior, and the "fading away" of some groups and their cultures may occur
as people vote with their feet, abandoning less successful groups and joining
more successful ones. If these preconditions exist, then cultural group selection certainly could occur.

But has it occurred? One possible example of the spread of an institution
because of cultural group selection might be the form of political organization known as the "state." The state, a centralized, hierarchical organization
that claims and enforces a monopoly on the legitimate use of force in a particular location, popped up several different times independently in human
prehistory. When early states did arise, they typically became more successful
than their decentralized neighbors, whom they quickly absorbed, displaced,
and sometimes even exterminated. On the other hand, a study of cultural
evolution in the New Guinea highlands suggests that while cultural group
selection may produce spectacular results when it does occur, like biological
group selection, it may be something of a rarity. The New Guinea study
shows that while groups do vary culturally, and hence behaviorally, it may be
unusual for between-group variations to last long enough or to have dramatic enough effects on the success of groups for cultural group selection to
work.[17] After all, when one group is dramatically more successful than its
neighbors, this typically is noticed and the reasons for the success inspire imitation. Such cultural diffusion is great for the success of the cultural trait involved, but reduces the between-group cultural differences necessary for us
to say "cultural group selection" has occurred.

Although memetics has produced some useful new insights and some sophisticated theorizing about the interactions between genes and cultural
traits in human evolution, it is still running on a track parallel to most of the
evolutionary biological study of human behavior. While cultural transmission remains an important area of research, studying how memes are spread
among people is still not quite the same thing as understanding the role of
culture in human behavior. The problem to be examined in the next chapter,
then, is how to accomplish the trick of looking at both things—behavior and
culture—at the same time, while still keeping ourselves within the evolutionary biological (i.e., scientific) study of our species.[18]

6

Of Missionaries and Mud

When an animal seeks to manipulate an inanimate object, it has only one recourse—physical power. A dung beetle can move a ball of dung only by forcibly pushing it. But when the object it seeks to manipulate is itself another live animal there is an alternative way. It can exploit the senses and muscles of the animal it is trying to control. . . .

—Richard Dawkins and John R. Krebs[1]

Eventually the guiding light at the end of my tunnel proved to be rhetoric, the notion that words and other performances are messages that can be used to manipulate other people.

—F. G. Bailey[2]

Unstung

As in most big cities, the streets of Nairobi are full of pickpockets, con artists, and other petty criminals. The con artists tend to hover near the big tourist hotels and outside cafes and shops in the busy, affluent center of town, looking for likely victims or "marks." One of their typical techniques is to sidle up next to tourists and ask, "How long have you been in Kenya?" If the answer is something like "two days," then the con begins. About ten years ago, my wife and I were nearly the marks of a very common con that went like this. A nicely dressed man asked us how long we had been in Kenya and whether we would like to chat and have a cup of tea. Suspecting a con, but having nothing better to do at the time, we accepted. Two of the man's friends soon appeared from out of nowhere, and they began to give us a sad story about how they were Ugandan students trapped in Kenya because of the troubles in Uganda at that time. If only they had some more money, they could go on with their studies! And so on. Fortunately for us, this was such an old con that we had already heard of it. Notices had been posted at the Nairobi Youth Hostel about the "Ugandan students" con game, though the particular nationality mentioned by the con artists has varied over the years according to which of Kenya's neighbors happened to be suffering from the worst political and economic instability at the moment. We refused to give them any money, endured some abuse about how cheap and selfish we were being, paid for the tea, and left.

What did culture have to do with that? In terms of memes and cultural transmission, not much. My wife and I did not become con artists, the con artists did not become marks, and very little in the way of culture was transmitted. Therefore the interaction is not of much interest to memeticists.[3] But encounters such as that one are, after all, quite common, and they do involve compelling human behaviors and evolved psychology. But if memetics doesn't have much to say about them, then how can we study them from an evolutionary framework while not neglecting the important role culture plays in them? After all, even though little in the way of memes is being transmitted in an encounter such as that between a con artist and his victim, the encounter does take a particular form because of the cultural context in which it occurs. This idea of culture as the context of human social interaction is an old one in cultural anthropology, and it forms the core of this chapter.

Back to the Beginning

For people such as me whose main concern is behavior itself, memetics has one major drawback: It pays very little attention to the relationship between culture and behavior. The only behavior of any real interest to a memeticist is one that transmits a meme. How those memes affect behavior is not a central concern. Indeed, from the point of view of memetics, it is precisely those memes that *don't* have much influence on behavior—so-called "ideal culture"—that are in many ways the most interesting and also perhaps the best at getting themselves copied. Imagine two memes, one that actually does influence behavior and another that spreads from person to person as a platitude more often ignored than observed. Which one is likely to be more successful? The one that actually influences behavior sticks its neck out and runs the risk of being selected against—people may decide that it amounts to a bad piece of advice—while the trait that simply passes from person to person with little effect on anything material is rarely put to any sort of practical test. These cultural traits might be analogous to commensal organisms, like many of the types of bacteria that ride along in our digestive tracts, deriving benefits from their hosts but, unlike parasitic organisms, doing no harm.

But culture that has little influence on behavior is not terribly interesting to those of us who are interested in behavior, and that brings us back to the problem of the relationship between culture and behavior. To many memeticists, that relationship is simple: Behavior is the product of culture. This is an old idea in the social sciences, and particularly in my discipline of anthropology. But, as we saw in Chapter 2, there are plenty of examples of human behavior that is *not* the product of culture. Furthermore, such a simple view of the relationship between culture and behavior has nothing to say about all of the discrepancies between behavior and culture described in Chapter 1. And if we can't deal with that problem, then we really are back to square one.

We might find a way out of this by carefully thinking about how exactly memes are transmitted from one person to another. Memeticists themselves have little to say about this. For them, it is sufficient to treat people as more or less passive recipients and transmitters of culture, paying little more attention to it than they pay to the burrs that stick to their socks or the cold viruses they pass on through sneezing. This is similar to the attitude geneticists take toward the details of biological reproduction. It is enough for them to know that genes do somehow get from one individual to another. The details of the mating rituals of a particular species or human society are really irrelevant. But, to someone interested in behavior, mating rituals and details of memetic transmission are important to study. Memes cannot spread just by themselves, and, unlike cold viruses, they do not usually spread from person to person without being changed a lot in the process. Some of the change has to do with the fact that culture traits are fairly low-fidelity replicators. Unlike DNA molecules, which almost never make mistakes when they copy themselves, culture traits are miscopied all the time, as anyone who has ever played the "telephone" game can tell you. Yet, a more interesting source of infidelity in the culture-copying process is introduced by the intentions, agendas, and creativity of people. What if we were to play the telephone game, in which a group of people in a room whisper a phrase to one another to see how the phrase changes by the time it reaches the end of the line—but allowing everyone to change the message in whatever way he or she wants? The message might be drastically changed from its original form not after being passed through a dozen or more individuals, but after just one. And that is what real life is like.

Engineering Culture

Culture traits are not like wild flu viruses, passed from person to person without modification. They are more akin to biological warfare viruses.

They are engineered, produced, and spread by evolved, self-interested organisms for strategic reasons. I do not try to pass a trait on to you because the trait tells me to. No one told me to write this book, for example. I did it because I wanted to change something about you, either the way you think or what you do. Intellectually, I want you to take seriously the evolutionary biology behind human behavior while also appreciating the role of culture in human affairs. More pragmatically, like any author I want you to think highly of me, to recommend the book to your friends, to recommend me for promotions and pay raises if you happen to be in a position to do so, and so on. I am trying to influence you with my message, and this is what all people do all the time, whether the message is "pass the salt" or "die for your country." Culture traits are continuously being reshaped, repackaged, and reused by individuals as they use them to deal with their social worlds. Most of the time this sort of cultural engineering is done on a small scale. I am doing it now, taking a few original ideas and a lot of borrowed ones, repackaging them and sending them out in an effort to influence the thoughts and actions of others. Occasionally, however, it is done on a grand scale, such as through government propaganda efforts or through the efforts of missionaries, who were often the official agents of colonial powers, to spread their religion. The biological warfare analogy retains the central idea behind all of memetics that culture consists of traits transmitted from one person to another and that can evolve in a way similar to other replicators, whether viruses or genes, but it also forces us to recognize the central role individuals play in this process of transmission.

Muddying the Waters

But there is still more to the role of culture in human social life than this. Even in encounters such as those between con artists and their marks, encounters in which little in the way of memes is being transmitted, culture is still there as the context of the interaction. A number of metaphors come to

mind. Culture is to human social life as water is to the lives of fishes or air is
to those of birds, it is the ever-present medium through which we must ma-
neuver to live, one of the raw materials we use in our efforts to deal with the
world, and so on. Just as fishes are particularly and finely adapted to life in
the water and birds are designed for life in the air, so are humans designed by
natural selection for a life in the medium of culture. But culture is not just an
obstacle in our path, it is also our main tool in life, the raw material out of
which we fashion ourselves and with which we influence others' opinions of
us. It is "material" in much the same sense as the "material" out of which we
make our clothing: It is the stuff in which we wrap ourselves to make ourselves more acceptable, presentable, influential, and attractive to others. Perhaps one could even say (after one has first inserted tongue in cheek) that
culture is to human social interaction as mud is to mud wrestling. Human
social life is a bit similar to wrestling in that it is so often a contest or struggle
between people with competing goals. But the addition of mud—culture—
drastically changes the nature of that struggle. Just as mud wrestlers are
coated in mud, people are coated in culture: It shapes who they are and how
they interact with others in very profound ways. Like mud, culture can get in
your eyes, leading you to do things that may not be in your own best interest. Just as mud wrestlers may use the mud itself in their contest—flinging it,
wallowing in it, using it to blind their opponents—so do people use culture
as a tool in social interaction. Just as one wrestler covered in mud is likely to
muddy others in the ring, so do culture traits cling to people and move from
one to another through social contact.

Folks such as me, who usually call ourselves human behavioral ecologists
or human evolutionary ecologists, have been studying human social interaction largely as if there were nothing else there—no water, no air, no clothing,
no mud, no culture. The memeticists, in contrast, have largely been studying
the properties of culture while ignoring the details of human social life. We
need to get beyond these limited approaches by looking closely at how people *use* culture in their efforts to deal with one another. Because the way that
people use culture in their interactions with one another is through communication, we will have to take a much closer look at the details of human
communication.

Communication and Culture

In short, culture is the raw material for the messages we send one another. As
a result, it is through communication that culture is made manifest and

available for study. The purpose of communication is to change what other people think and do—in a technical sense, to *manipulate* them. It is not necessarily a bad thing to be "manipulated" in this sense. If I shout at you to step out of the path of an oncoming truck, surely I am attempting to manipulate you, and surely you should be grateful to me for having done so. There is nothing necessarily selfish or Machiavellian about the word "manipulation" when it is used in this technical way.

The advantages of this approach are easy to see when we consider the discrepancies between culture and behavior described in Chapter 1. Unlike naive cultural determinism and some of the models of the memeticists, it does not assume that behavior is simply a product of culture or that there will be any simple correspondence between behavior and culture. Unlike E. B. Tylor's old catch-all definition of culture, it does not simply redefine behavior as culture. Instead, it treats culture and behavior as two separate though closely related things, acknowledging the gap between what people say and what they do. If people say what they say for reasons other than a desire to enlighten their listeners about their attitudes and intentions, then there is no longer any reason to expect a simple correspondence between statements and actions or between culture and behavior. "Statements" and "culture" are not the same, but for the most part what has been enshrined in thousands of ethnographies as "culture" is primarily based on what people say, and very often on what they say publicly. Given the pressure of public opinion and people's desires to enhance their reputations and to manipulate the behavior of others, public statements may be very bad places to look for clues as to how people actually behave. Lies are just one extreme form this sort of manipulative communication can take.

Unlike the idea that achievement of cultural success should correlate with biological success, this idea does not lead to the prediction that achievement of what is culturally valued will necessarily lead anyone to have more children. After all, the "culturally defined" values that an outsider finds easiest to record, and so are most likely to be enshrined in ethnographies as the culture of a particular group, are those values that are loudly and publicly expressed ("Young men ought to go off and fight in wars," "men should not attempt to have sex with the king's wives," and so on). Those sorts of very public values may have more to do with manipulating people in ways that are good for the speaker than with enlightening them about the best way for them to live. The sorts of admonitions and advice that really would help someone get ahead in life may be more likely to be expressed quietly and privately, perhaps often from parent to child, and so may be recorded much more seldom by ethnographers.[4]

Why We're So Smart

This approach to culture and communication is in much the same spirit as some recently developed ideas about the evolution of intelligence and the development of moral systems. Not long ago, the standard line in anthropology was that the evolution of human intelligence had everything to do with tool use. Ours hands were freed by walking upright, giving us the capacity to use tools, and little by little our brains grew to meet this challenge and opportunity. This is a seductive line of thought, particularly when almost all we have to go on when reconstructing the evolution of human intelligence is the tools our ancestors left behind. But it is quite possible that we are unnecessarily impressed with our own tool-using abilities. How elaborate, for example, would our tools be if we had to reinvent them with every generation? Or, even worse, if each individual had to reinvent them him or herself? Some of us certainly would figure out simple things such as how to sharpen a stick or how to produce a sharp edge on a rock, but it is doubtful that we would get much beyond that if we were not so social. And being social opens the door to socially transmitted information: culture. We certainly are good at making and using tools, but perhaps we owe that less to our innate abilities as tinkerers and more to our sociality and our ability to create and share new ideas.

If that is the case, then the key to human intelligence may be sociality itself. This hypothesis was first proposed by Nicholas Humphrey, who suggested that what human brains are really designed for is dealing with our complex social world.[5] Consider, Humphrey writes, Robinson Crusoe. At first he is alone on his desert island, and he faces all sorts of environmental and technical problems. Things were tough, but they really became complicated when Friday arrived on the scene. "If Monday and Tuesday, Wednesday, and Thursday had turned up as well then Crusoe would have had every need to keep his wits about him." Other people are so complex that to deal with them effectively, we have to build models in our minds of what is going on in theirs. We are so good at this that it strikes most of us as nothing extraordinary, but the complexity of the mental operations involved is truly astounding. And our ability to do this seems to be something that really does set us apart, by degree if not by kind, from all other species. Chimpanzees show some ability to know what is going on in other chimpanzees' minds, as do some other primates, but their abilities are quite limited compared to ours.[6]

Human intelligence seems to be especially keen when social situations are involved, but, apart from a few people concentrated in math departments and chess clubs, we are not so good at abstract problem solving. Consider, for example, an abstract version of a logical problem known as the Wason selection task: You have been given a new clerical job at a high school, and you are asked to make sure that students' documents conform to this rule: "If a person has a 'D' rating, then his documents must be marked code '3.'" If you are presented with cards labeled "D," "F," "3," and "7," which cards do you absolutely have to turn over to determine whether the rule is being followed? Typically, less than a quarter of the people who are asked this question choose the correct answer: cards "D" and "7" (Here's the reasoning: You need to check the "D" card to make sure there is a "3" on the other side, and you need to check the "7" card to make sure that it is not a mislabeled "D" card, but the rule says nothing about "F" cards and it does not violate the rule if some other letter is also coded as "3," so you do not need to look at either of them). But if the same abstract reasoning problems are rephrased in terms of social rules ("Are these people breaking a social rule? If so, nail them!"), then suddenly the average person's score improves dramatically. Consider this logical problem: You have been given the task of cracking down on underage drinking in a bar by enforcing the rule "If a person is drinking beer, then he must be over 20 years old." The information you have to work with is on cards, with each person's age printed on one side and what he or she is drinking printed on the other. If you are presented with cards labeled "drinking beer," "drinking coke," "25 years old," and "16 years old," which cards must you turn over to determine whether the law is being followed? In this case, typically about three quarters of the people asked choose the correct answer: the cards labeled "drinking beer" and "16 years old." This is logically identical to the question about the cards given above. It was once thought that the difference in people's success rates on these two questions was simply an effect of the familiarity people had with the subject matter, but it has been shown that that is not the case. Even when the same exact logical problem is phrased in terms of a strange, arbitrary social rule in an exotic and alien cultural setting, people's success rates are high. The key difference is that in one case it is phrased as an abstract problem, while in the other case it is phrased in terms of the enforcement of a social rule, and this appears to be something that we are particularly good at doing.[7]

Why We're So Moral

More broadly, the human need to keep track of others' behavior may also help to explain the development of moral systems—codes each society has of "right" behavior. Moral systems may have their origins in what is called "indirect reciprocity." Indirect reciprocity involves an audience. In "direct" reciprocity, I do something nice for you because I think there is a good chance that you will some day return the favor. In "indirect" reciprocity, I do something nice for you even if you are totally incapable of returning the favor, because someone else may be watching, and I may be able to get a reputation as an especially nice, "moral" guy who helps his fellow man in need.[8]

This idea may explain the fundamentally selfish logic behind acting unselfishly at times, but it does not give an accurate idea of the motivations that people usually feel when they follow moral codes. Most people, most of the time, internalize moral codes, following their dictates because they honestly feel that it is the "right" thing to do. It may be that the social pressure for and long-term advantages of such "moral" behavior may be so great that internalizing moral codes and following them even when it is a costly thing to do may be the best long-run policy for most people. And the costliness of the behavior may be just the thing that other people may be primed to examine most closely. This "costly-to-fake" or "handicap" principle may be illustrated with the example of a college degree with honors from an elite university. Although plenty of smart, hard-working people graduate each year without honors and from ordinary universities, an employer looking for a smart, hard-working person may still look for those with honors from elite universities because such a behavior is costly to fake. If a person were not really smart and hard working, he or she would have a difficult time accomplishing the task of completing a degree with honors at an elite university. Or consider the history of lace in European clothing. Between the sixteenth and eighteenth centuries, lace was handmade, very expensive, and widely used. When lace-making machines were introduced in the nineteenth century, its price dropped, and, after an initial large increase, eventually so did its use. This may have been because lace lost its value as a reliable signal. When lace was handmade and expensive, it was a signal of wealth and anyone looking for a wealthy person would do well to look for lacy clothing. When it became cheap, anyone could wear it, and so no one did—it no longer communicated anything important.[9]

And if those two examples don't convince you, perhaps this one will. This same principle is at the heart of one of my children's favorite stories, *The Sneetches* by Dr. Seuss. As you might expect from Dr. Seuss, Sneetches live on beaches, and they come in two kinds: those with stars on their bellies and those without. At the story's outset, belly stars are reliable and hard to fake signs of high status. Star-belly Sneetches enjoy the privileges of elite group membership (namely, frankfurter parties and marshmallow toasts), while plain-belly Sneetches are excluded. But then along comes Sylvester McMonkey McBean, who offers to put stars—indistinguishable from the kind with which some Sneetches are born—on the bellies of plain-belly Sneetches. Soon, when every Sneetch on the beach has a star, McBean produces his star-off machine, and having no star becomes, very temporarily, the sign of high status. And so on. Eventually, after all of the Sneetches have spent all of their money, McBean leaves, and the Sneetches finally realize that a belly star—or the lack of one—does not say much of anything about the individual Sneetch behind it.[10]

If the star-belly principle were the only thing influencing communication, then we would expect only honest signals. Any signal that was cheap and easy to fake would be ignored, and only costly, honest signals would receive any attention. Clearly, that is not the case, either among humans or nonhumans. Even if most of us are not ready to agree with one cynical observer that "human society is a network of lies and deception,"[11] we are all quite aware of the ubiquity of deception in our own species, and examples from the nonhuman world are abundant as well. The problem may be that it is not always easy or cheap for signal receivers to detect deception.[12] In some cases, the very characteristics of a signal that make it believable, such as its duration or variety, also make it expensive for the receiver to measure. Because of the sometimes high costs of detecting deception, selection may favor receivers who settle for less informative signals that are also less costly to receive. This may help to explain why dishonest signals seem to be so common. For instance, if a female bird has to spend a lot of valuable time and risk her life to compare a lot of potential mates, then her best strategy may be to forego the search and mate with a male that is readily available and that appears to be at least fairly good. Humans also encounter this dilemma all the time, most obviously when shopping. If your time for shopping is short (or if, like me, you hate to shop), then you may decide to go ahead and buy something whose good looks may be deceptive because it is simply too costly to keep searching for the best possible choice. Some things, such as my old coffee maker that looked so good in the store but that I soon gave away in frustration and replaced with one recommended by a friend, are almost impossible to assess without first consuming them. Books and movies are two more examples of this problem. Whether or not a particular book is worth its cover price or a movie is worth the admission price is hard to know without first paying for it. This is frustrating news for consumers, but, to look on the bright side, it means that those of us who like to study the use of deceptive signals in society won't be running out of subject matter any time soon.

And Why We Talk So Much

Language deserves some special attention because it is, after all, the medium of so much cultural transmission and so many of our efforts at manipulation and persuasion. Language is also a ripe fruit for any biocultural approach to try to pick because of how it involves biology—the hard-wired circuitry of our brains that makes language possible—and culture. Fortunately, this approach is in harmony with some new ideas about the origins of language and its role in human evolution. For example, it has been suggested that the key role of language in human evolution was its usefulness as a sort of social glue.[13] The "glue" of nonhuman primate societies is social grooming. Primates groom each other not only to keep themselves free of ticks, lice, and other pests, but also to keep in touch—literally—with one another. It is a way of helping one another, reassuring one another, and keeping tabs on one another. But grooming has its limits as a form of social glue. Larger groups have many advantages over smaller groups, including better predator defense, better effectiveness as predators, and perhaps also better defense against competing groups of one's species, and there is evidence that the size of the groups our ancestors lived in increased over evolutionary time along with their brain sizes.

However, as the size of a social group goes up, so does the amount of time each individual must spend grooming. Eventually, it becomes a burden. While gelada baboons, which have the highest recorded grooming rate of any nonhuman primate, spend about 20 percent of their time grooming one another, it has been estimated that humans living in groups of about 150 individuals would have to spend between one third and one half of their time grooming, if that were the way they kept tabs on one another. Language may have taken the place of grooming as our species' social glue. And, indeed, we use language in many of the same ways that nonhuman primates use grooming: to keep in touch with one another, to reassure one another, to help one another, and, of course, to manipulate one another.

If the glue of a human society is its language, will just any language do the job? While all languages are good at communicating, that is not the only job of a language. Paradoxically, another purpose of language is precisely the opposite: to make communication difficult. As anyone who has tried to learn a foreign language—or even another accent of one's own language—can easily attest, after childhood, it is very difficult to learn another language so well that one can pass as a native speaker. As with a belly star to a Sneetch, a language that is fully mastered only by native speakers is an excellent marker of group membership, and so languages, dialects, and accents form reliable markers of group identity. This may help to explain why so many languages are so complex and arcane and why even minor variations in accents among speakers of the same language can be so difficult to master. As a Yankee living in Texas for ten years now, I can attest to the fact that it is difficult to tackle even a mildly different local dialect. I am only now beginning to incorporate a few "y'all"s and "fixin' to"s into my daily speech. This also helps me to understand why the Maasai language is so difficult. When I mention the complexity of Maasai, which, like many African languages, is tonal and has an amazingly complicated verbal system, students often ask why people with such simple technology should have such a complex language. The answer is that linguistic complexity has little or nothing to do with technological or social complexity but a lot to do with the use of the language to clearly define a social group. Languages used to communicate between groups, including pidgins, creoles, and the "bush" Swahili spoken by many in the East African interior, are typically relatively simple and easy to master. Even very small groups have a tendency to develop dialects peculiar to them that help them to distinguish group members from nongroup members. My wife and I, for instance, both speak English as our first language and have some knowledge of several other languages as well, and much of our conversation consists of words and phrases from those languages put together in odd ways that no one besides the two of us could possibly understand. For instance, only those few people who have some knowledge of Swahili and Spanish will be able to translate the word *ninaducha*.

Looking for a *Suaböya* in All the Wrong Places

Ideas such as these are fascinating and should be the inspiration of future research on the details of human social life and communication. But there already exist a few good examples of how people use culture as the raw material of the signals they apply to their day-to-day social interactions. My favorite example comes from the Yanomamö Indians of Venezuela and Brazil—an example that requires a brief detour into the arcane and complex world of kinship terminologies and marriage rules.[14]

The Yanomamö, as with many other peoples, have a prescriptive rule of bilateral cross-cousin marriage that is expressed in their Iroquois-style kinship terminology. What all of this anthropologese means is just this: A man must marry a woman of his own genealogical generation who is either his mother's brother's daughter or his father's sister's daughter, or a more distant cousin for whom he uses the same kinship term, *suaböya*. *Suaböya* means, simultaneously, "cross-cousin" (i.e., a cousin linked by a brother and a sister, rather than by a pair of brothers or a pair of sisters), "wife," "potential wife," and "sister-in-law" (because a man might marry her sister rather than her, or one of his brothers might marry her instead). A Yanomamö man uses the term *suaböya* for all women that he may marry under this rule, regardless of whether he actually marries them. Parallel cousins (father's brother's daughters, mother's sister's daughters, and more distant cousins in the same category) are prohibited as marriage partners, and they are called "brother" and "sister." Thus, for a man to marry his parallel cousin would be "incestuous" because she is his "sister." Marriages between people of different genealogical generations (uncles, aunts, nieces, nephews, and so on) are also considered incestuous and are prohibited. This may seem a bizarre system, but it is quite common, and quite an everyday thing for millions of people.

Such a system obviously creates a bit of a problem for many men: What if there are no *suaböya* around to marry? This problem is likely to occur because, first, the Yanomamö are polygynous, so many of the available women may already be married, and, second, genealogical generations do not always match up well with chronological ages. Someone a man calls *suaböya* may be too young or too old to marry. This mismatch between chronological and genealogical ages happens in our society, too, occasionally, as when a nephew or niece is older than his or her aunt or uncle because the parents have continued to reproduce even after they have a grandchild. In a society such as the Yanomamö, where men continue reproducing into old age and women start as soon as they are physically able, routinely becoming grandmothers in their 30s, this is an even more common problem.

The solution to the Yanomamö men's problem lies in that they are often related to others in more than one way. This will inevitably happen in societies where it is normal to marry relatives. Some Yanomamö are related to each other in as many as seven different ways. The "official rule" is that when deciding what kin term to use for someone, one is supposed to use the term that refers to the closest relationship one has with the person. But this rule is easily and often fudged. It may be that a man is supposed to call a particular girl "niece" or even "daughter," but perhaps through some other series of kin links she fits into the *suaböya* category. This is precisely what Yanomamö men do. When Yanomamö men are asked what they call various women in their communities, they usually follow the rules and place women into the categories associated with their closest genealogical link. But a significant proportion of the time, they move women from one category to another, and more often than not, they move women from categories they could not marry—"daughter," "niece," and so on—to the *suaböya* category. Most of the women they move in this way are the younger ones, not the older ones, which reinforces the impression that this is part of a strategy for obtaining more mates. They also tend to move women into the "mother-in-law" category, which may seem odd. Why would anyone want *more* mothers-in-law? But by moving older women into that category, they are by implication moving those women's daughters into the *suaböya* category. Other Yanomamö men do not necessarily sit idly by while other men move women into inaccessible categories, however. Arguments and fights over which matches are incestuous and which are allowed are common. Interestingly, an element of nepotism creeps into such controversies: Yanomamö are less likely to label marriages by their close relatives as incestuous than those of distant relatives.

This is an excellent example of how an existing cultural code is manipulated for reproductive benefit, which makes it easy to tie it all in with an evolutionary approach. But kin-term manipulation may be a much more widespread phenomenon. For example, such phrases as "Brother, can you spare a dime" may be attempts to exploit the expectation of benevolence among kin, and the use of kin terms in political speech ("fatherland," "motherland," "brothers and sisters," "founding fathers," and so on) may be attempts to manipulate others because we all evolved in societies in which authority figures were mainly kin. Furthermore, such simple rhetorical tactics may actually be effective in persuading voters. In a recent study, subjects listened to one of three versions of a political campaign speech, one using kin terms such as "brothers and sisters," another using the terms "friend" and "friends," and another using terms such as "fellow citizens." Those who listened to the versions using the kin terms reported significantly higher levels of agreement with the speaker's position after hearing the speech than those who listened to either of the other versions.[15]

All in the Family

This approach might help to make sense of the many things people say that appear to run counter to the logic of evolutionary theory. Consider, for instance, men's rhetoric about women in New Guinea highland societies.[16] Men in much of New Guinea will go on and on about the risks of associating with women, arguing that not only sex but almost any form of contact with women is dangerous and polluting, and, in some societies in the area, encouraging male homosexuality. Menstrual blood is often said to be an extraordinarily powerful and evil poison. Women are depicted as dangerous temptresses, and the virtuous man is the one able to resist the temptations of premarital and adulterous sex. If they genuinely believe that women are dangerous to associate with and behave in accordance with this belief, then presumably they are routinely passing up opportunities to mate and reproduce. Where is the sense in that? But perhaps these sorts of statements should not be taken at face value. It may be that such teachings are attempts by males to manipulate their reproductive competitors.

Another common cultural belief that makes little obvious sense in terms of the logic of adaptation is the idea that children have a moral obligation to help support their aged parents. Such a belief has been recorded time and time again all over the globe. It is often used as an explanation for why people in less economically developed societies tend to have many children (i.e., they are a sort of primitive, old-age security scheme). Often this idea is enshrined in colorful folk tales that are assumed to reflect the deep tendencies of the culture at hand. The Maasai, for example, have a saying that "he who has children does not sleep in the bush." The Bible admonishes offspring to "honor thy father and thy mother." And the Chinese constitution declares that "Parents have the duty to rear and educate their minor children, and children who have come of age have the duty to support and assist their parents." And a recent survey of American parents revealed that the value they most want to convey to their children—more than patriotism, diligence, or consideration of others—is respect for the elderly. Such beliefs present a problem for the evolutionary biological approach to human behavior: How can they be so common when it is not clear how natural selection could have favored the evolution of an organism that routinely lived long enough to become a burden on its own offspring? Why do all peoples not leave their old people to die on ice floes, or the local equivalent? Have we reached the limit of evolutionary biology's relevance to human behavior, or is something else going on? The possibility exists that, far from being simple, straightforward reflections of peoples' feelings and intentions, such statements are actually attempts to manipulate the behavior of others.

The manipulation could work in at least two ways. First, children could be attempting to manipulate their parents. It is cheap for children to promise old-age support since death rates in traditional societies make the necessity of actually having to pay it unlikely, but such promises may have the benefit of keeping benefits from parents flowing. In this case, one would expect adults with living parents to be the individuals who most enthusiastically and loudly proclaim the importance of children's obligation to provide support for their parents in old age. One would also expect such adults whose parents have a great deal to offer in the way of inheritable property to be more vocal about their intentions than those who stand to inherit little.

Second, parents could be attempting to manipulate their children. If so, then statements about the obligation of children to support their parents should be most frequently and loudly reiterated by parents in situations where such support is in the greatest doubt, perhaps because the parents have little to offer their adult children in exchange. This interpretation is supported by some folk wisdom on the subject. For example, although among Indian peasants all children are exhorted to help support their elderly parents, it is well known that, as an Indian man once said to a demographer, "Without property, children do not look after their parents well."[17] Similarly, in another Indian village, while landowners generally felt secure that their sons would provide old-age support for them, poor men were pessimistic about their children's magnanimity.[18] Why would it be adaptive for parents to manipulate their children in this way? The answer is that it may not be. Such statements may simply reflect the general human desire to remain alive and healthy, a motivation so powerfully adaptive throughout most of life that it may be hard to turn off suddenly in old age.[19]

Rashomon in the Bush

Studying how culture is used as the context and medium of human social interaction will require some creativity on the part of researchers, especially if we want to be able to systematically test hypotheses in rigorous ways. Anthropologists and fans of classic foreign films are familiar with something called the Rashomon effect, named after a film by the Japanese director Akira Kurosawa. The film's plot is based on a short story by the early twentieth-century Japanese author Ryunosuke Akutagawa, though the title is taken from another of his works. In Akutagawa's and Kurosawa's renditions, different witnesses to an event tell different versions of the same story, with each version portraying the teller in the best light. Although anthropologists have noticed the Rashomon effect in discrepancies among different informants' versions of the truth and among different ethnographers' interpretations of a particular culture, their usual position has long been that although Rashomon effects can be interesting, the ultimate goal of the ethnographer is not to dwell on such discrepancies but to find ways to resolve them, to create a picture of a culture as a coherent and unified whole. For anyone interested in social strategies, however, it is the discrepancies between different informants' accounts themselves that are most important to examine.

The questions to ask when faced with such discrepancies are obvious. First, what do the various people stand to gain from their versions? In the case of the film *Rashomon*, the advantages to each character are clear. A bandit presents himself as seductive and heroic, a woman presents herself as virtuous and faithful to her husband, and so on. If only real-world situations permitted such simple interpretations, researchers would have it easy. Yet, by deliberately seeking out individuals who may be predicted to have different perspectives on events because of their different situations in life, researchers should be able to identify and interpret such Rashomon-type effects. Anyone who has ever been married would be able to predict, for instance, that husbands and wives often see things quite differently. Sociologists have been able to quantify the divergence between husbands' and wives' views of a sensitive domestic issue: Who takes care of the little chores that keep the family running, from child discipline to meal preparation to home repairs? Not surprisingly, the wives were two to three times as likely as the husbands to report that the wives were the ones who dealt with such tasks.[20]

Everyone is also quite familiar with the logical opposite of the Rashomon effect, the audience effect. While the Rashomon effect involves variations between informants' statements when there is one interviewer and several informants, the audience effect involves variations in statements from a single informant when he is exposed to different audiences. Similar to the Rashomon effect, the audience effect is common in everyday life. For example, job seekers tailor their resumes to suit different positions, emphasizing one specialty in one case and another in another case in an attempt to manipulate those doing the hiring. Scholars often take the same basic research and publish it several times, reshaping it to suit different audiences. The audience effect has also been observed by fieldworkers, although most commonly it is seen as a problem, not a source of new insights. For example, the main ethnographer of the Yanomamö, Napoleon Chagnon, found that only by being the sole member of the audience when conducting genealogical interviews with his Yanomamö informants could he hope to get accurate information from them.[21] Sometimes, however, audience effects can reveal how a society really works. Consider, for instance, the discrepancies between what subordinate people say when they are alone and what they say when members of the elite are present. One such subordinate group, Malay peasants, often work as harvesters for wealthy neighbors and routinely receive a bonus in grain in addition to their wage. The wealthy call this bonus *zakat*, a sort of Islamic tithe that enhances one's reputation for generosity and piety. Publicly, the harvesters accept that name for it, while privately they argue that it

was simply their due and not *zakat* at all.[22] Closer to home, Scott Adams'
Dilbert comic strip gives voice to the frustrations of modern cubicle workers,
including wonderful satires of idiotic bosses and their lame-brained theories
of management, revealing sentiments that most employees would never
openly express with their bosses present. An Ethiopian proverb eloquently
summarizes the importance of audience effects: "When the great lord passes
the wise peasant bows deeply and silently farts."[23]

Although audience effects can sometimes be discerned in the natural
course of everyday social life, it also might be a good idea to seek them out in
a more deliberate way. One way is to vary the identity of the interviewer by
using assistants. Assistants can be males or females, young or old, educated
or not, high status or low status, members of the group under study or out-
siders. The best ways to vary the characteristics of the interviewers will depend on the specifics of the research situation.[24] Another way to elicit audience effects would be to vary the settings of interviews, conducting some
privately with no audiences and conducting others in groups, varying the
people present in ways that are meaningful given the topic being explored.
For example, a person studying the possibility that children manipulate their
parents by making promises of old age support would need to vary the ages
and the sorts of relatives present in different interviews.

Yanomamö kin-term usage presents an interesting opportunity to explore
audience effects. Would the mens' answers to questions about what they call
various relatives vary according to the audience present at the interview?
Would they more likely push the bounds of propriety and use terms such as
suaböya in questionable cases when alone with the interviewer or when only
close kin are present, and would they avoid such usages when competing
males are present? Would males more likely reclassify females when their audience consists of males of lower status than when their audience consists of
competing males of higher status? And what about those New Guinea men
who talk so much about the dangers of women? If those sorts of statements
are indeed intended to manipulate sexual competitors, then the loudest,
most conspicuous and repetitive signals should be used by men when they
are dealing with their direct reproductive competitors. When men are speaking privately with their close kinsmen, more muted, economical, and truth-
ful signals, perhaps including private confessions that women may not be so
bad after all, ought to be used. Something like this may be happening among
the Gahuku of New Guinea's Eastern Highlands, where, although men show
deep public concern about the dangers posed by women, in private young
men are also instructed in how to seduce them.[25]

This view of culture as something that is routinely subject to manipulation for essentially selfish ends may also have ethical and moral implications. Although it is tempting to view other peoples' cultures as sacrosanct and off limits to our ethical judgment, this is a difficult position to adhere to if much of what we know of other peoples' cultures consists of, for want of a better word, propaganda. Fortunately, as I hope to show in the next chapter, this is a problem that we can deal with.

7

Gardening Tips

The final chapter is where, by tradition, the author attempts to demonstrate how all that went before can solve social problems, improve morality, make one a more effective competitor, or in some other manner contribute to making life better for us all. Now that we have a framework for understanding the evolution of the human mind and of culture, are we better off? Do we have the basis for a science of social engineering?

—Jerome Barkow [1]

In the spring of 1996, two stories made American headlines. The first concerned a young woman named Fauziya Kassindja from the West African country of Togo.[2] She had fled her country a year and a half earlier to avoid genital mutilation and an arranged marriage, only to spend her time in the United States subjected to dehumanizing treatment in a series of detention centers and prisons while she waited for a hearing on her request for asylum. The other concerned the FBI's capture of Theodore Kaczynski, age 53, a loner from the Montana backwoods, on suspicion of being the "Unabomber," a mysterious figure who had spent seventeen years terrorizing the nation by sending carefully crafted letter bombs to academics and others involved with the development of industrial technology.

It would be hard to find two people any more different than Kassindja and Kaczynski or any two more unrelated news stories. Perhaps the only characteristic that their stories do share is that they hold lessons for the subject of this chapter: What might be the practical benefits of the approach advocated in this book, an approach seeking insights into human behavior by looking at the dance between culture and our shared, evolved human nature? In short, what good will this approach do us as social engineers? The experiences of Kassindja and other women like her provide an example of how the abuse of the culture concept can result in the rights of culture being elevated above the rights of people, while Kaczynski is a symptom of just how much modern society and culture have diverged from those that fostered the evolution of our shared human nature.

"Social engineering" is an ugly and frightening phrase to many people, but, like so many of the ideas discussed in this book, it is only a metaphor. "Social gardening" would be every bit as apt a way to describe the efforts of people to alter, in big and little ways, their behavior, the behavior of others, and the institutional frameworks in which they all live. Even those of us who prefer the decentralized, naturalistic, bottoms-up approach of an English-style social garden to the rigid lines and neatly trimmed hedges of the French style are still advocating a type of gardening, at a minimum, a set of policies favoring some sorts of behaviors and social arrangements over others. Although as a scientist I am a strong advocate of knowledge for its own sake, I also recognize that for many people this is not enough. For them, science must justify itself not just in terms of the intellectual satisfaction it provides scientists, but by the practical benefits it provides everyone else.

Tolerating the Intolerable

Let's begin by looking at the practical benefits provided by one alternative: cultural determinism. What practical good has the average person received from the doctrine that culture is the only significant influence on human behavior? It can be argued, with some justification, that when the culturalist approach was new it was a key element in the argument against racism in particular and against the broader idea that biology is destiny. In the intellectual milieu of the early twentieth century, it was a major step forward. Nativist and racist doctrines of the inherent superiority of Whites in general, and of northern Europeans in particular, were rampant and were fueled in the United States by alarm over growing rates of immigration mainly from Eastern and Southern Europe. In response to arguments that such immigrants were watering down America's good Anglo-Saxon stock, Franz Boas, the founder of academic anthropology in the United States, conducted a key piece of research, showing that although immigrants' physical forms, particularly the shapes of their heads, may have varied from the American average on arrival, their children's bodies and head shapes showed a definite shift toward the American pattern.[3] Not only was biology not destiny as far as behavior was concerned, in this case it was not even destiny for the development of the human body!

Research such as this, along with ethnographies that revealed the wisdom and logic behind the customs of culturally different peoples, set the stage for the tremendous advances in race relations, such as the desegregation of schools and armed forces, that followed World War II, as well as for the widespread interest in cultural diversity that has bloomed in the late twentieth century. As an anthropologist and as a citizen of the world, I consider these accomplishments to be enormous and, I hope, pivotal in human history. Before the development of the culture concept, only two explanations were given for the behavior of people different from oneself: ignorance or stupidity. The first left open the possibility that these others could be taught the "correct" way to behave; the second did not. It is a privilege to be part of the discipline that made such explanations unacceptable.

Perhaps because the doctrine of cultural relativism has had such an admirable history in terms of its influence on our social lives, there has been a tendency in recent years to take it a bit too far, to allow an idea that began simply as the scientist's disinterested detachment from his subject to slide into moral relativism. College students in particular tend to be relativistic and tolerant to a fault. When I have raised the issue of cultural relativism in my own classes, some students—students with otherwise mainstream political and moral opinions—have earnestly used the idea of "culture" to exonerate the efforts of the Nazis to exterminate European Jewry. "It's *their* culture, so who are *we* to judge it?" is the reasoning offered, implicitly putting the Holocaust on the same moral level as eating bratwurst.

The same sort of radical relativism has stymied the efforts of Fauziya Kassindja and other African women who have sought asylum in the United States because of the threat and promise of female circumcision in their homelands. Although the practice of female circumcision is becoming more widely known in the West, most people in our society are not clear on what it entails. The name is really a euphemism. To call it "circumcision" is to call what Lorena Bobbit did to her husband John "circumcision."[4] While the male operation involves only the removal of the foreskin, the female operation is usually much more drastic. While in some societies it involves only a ceremonial knick of the hood covering the clitoris, in most cases it involves anything ranging from removal of the clitoris to removal of the clitoris and some or all of the labia minora, to removal of the clitoris and labia minora and sewing up the opening, leaving only a small passage for menstrual blood and urine. In some societies it is performed on babies and young girls, while others, including the Mukogodo and other Maasai-speakers, wait until a girl has had her first menses. It is a common practice in some parts of Africa and the Middle East, though even in the West removal of the clitoris was used by a few physicians in the nineteenth century to control women thought to have an excessive interest in sex.[5] My wife, Beth Leech, is one of the few Westerners to have seen a female circumcision. Here are her field notes, reproduced here with only minor editing to preserve the privacy of those mentioned, from the first of two circumcisions she witnessed in 1986, one that involved a girl from an ethnic group neighboring the Mukogodo who was preparing to marry a man from yet another neighboring group:

> Arrived at the settlement just before 6:00 A.M. Still dark out. Stood at gate and a girl saw me, greeted me, and asked me why I was there. I told her for the circumcision, so she said, "Let's go" and led me through the settlement to her mother's house. Outside the house, dressed in a white cloak, was Natito, her head freshly shaved. With her was a girl about her age dressed in a school uniform. Natito asked if I had brought a knife. I didn't understand except literally, so said quizzically, "You want a knife? No, I don't have one." Later I heard her ask others the same question and figured out that it was rhetorical and meant to show that she wasn't afraid. By about 6:10 several girls had gathered and Natito's aunt came up and told us, "Sing now." So the girls, including Natito and I, stood up by the side of the house and began to sing. Natito's older sister and Natito were among the song leaders. After we'd sung for a while, the leaders stopped. During a several-minute silence, tears filled the eyes of Natito's older sister, and Natito and several others seemed to be trying to force tears to their eyes. Some young brides and young mothers came up and we began to sing again, sometimes with one of them leading. Mostly just the girls sang, although a young married woman would occasionally lead a verse.
>
> About 6:30 Natito's aunt said, "Now." The girls and young women joined the old women a few steps away outside the door of the house. A hide was brought out of the house and arranged in the doorway. The men now all were outside the settlement. Another lady brought a pot of water. The pot looked like it hadn't been washed—like there was cooked-on porridge around the edges. The lady took a spearhead out of the water and put it on top of the house. Natito was led onto the hide. She removed her white cape and stood naked on the hide, her body shielded from the view of men outside by a semicircle of women and girls. Cold water from the pot was poured over Natito's head. She shivered. More water was splashed on her body, and the pot was set down on the edge of the hide. Natito kicked it angrily (part of the ceremony) all over me (not part of the ceremony). Natito then sat on the hide, facing me, arms akimbo, legs bent and spread. Her aunt holds one of her shoulders; three

other women hold the other shoulder and her two legs. The circumcision lady unwrapped her razorblade and the operation began. All I can see is the woman's butt and the squinched-up face of Natito. She does not cry or cry out, just squinches her face tighter and tighter. Her aunt kept saying the equivalent of "Come on, that's right, chin up, you're almost done, brave girl, you can do it, come on." The lady's butt moved aside and I could see her fingering the bloody area, moving the lips aside. It was as if the clitoris was a plant: she had cut the stem and now must dig out the root. The women and girls crowded closer, watching every movement. Within two minutes it was over. The mother brought a gourd of milk from the house. A woman poured milk in the lid, allowing the milk to splatter onto the ground and onto what was left of Natito's genitals. Sheep fat was then smeared, globbed over the wound. Natito was then picked up under the arms and by the legs and carried into the house. On the hide I could see about a pint of Natito's blood, mixed with milk. She still had not cried out, but as they carried her in, her eyes were wet and her breath came in high wheezes. As Natito was carried in, another woman carried in the hide, folding it in half and lifting up the ends to keep in the blood and milk. An old woman picked up a broom of branches and swept the doorway clean.

Natito was married the next day.

A strict application of the logic of cultural relativism would lead us to tolerate and even support this practice, despite how reluctant we might be to have it performed on ourselves, our daughters, our sisters, or our wives. This is the position taken by John F. Gossart, Jr., an immigration judge in Baltimore. In refusing the asylum claim of a woman from Sierra Leone in 1995, Judge Gossart described female circumcision as "an important ritual" that "binds the tribe," noting that "while some cultures view FGM [female genital mutilation] as abhorrent and/or even barbaric, others do not." The woman from Sierra Leone, he said, "cannot change that she is a female, but she can change her mind with regards to her position toward the FGM practices. It is not beyond [her] control to acquiesce to the tribal position on FGM."[6] Not all immigration judges take similar positions. Judge Paul Nejelsky of Arlington, Virginia, ruled in favor of the asylum claim of another woman from Sierra Leone, arguing that "forced female genital mutilation clearly merits being recognized as a form of persecution."[7]

Absolutist Alternatives

Explaining behavior and justifying behavior are two very different things. Although one of the central arguments of this book is that culture is overused as an explanation for behavior, it is still a perfectly good and legitimate explanation in many, many cases. Yet, to move from using culture as an explanation of behavior to using it as a moral justification for behavior in the style of radical relativists like Judge Gossart is to slide from an "is" statement to an "ought" statement, a violation of a principle laid down convincingly by the Scottish philosopher David Hume more than two centuries ago.[8] Ironically, many of those who are quick to justify and defend others' behaviors on cultural grounds also denounce biological approaches to behavior because they imagine that biological explanations might be used to justify unsavory, antisocial behaviors. To do so is to commit what is often called the "naturalistic fallacy," the idea that if something is "natural" it must therefore be "good."[9] This sort of logic may work for granola, but it does not work for behavior. There may be biological reasons for jealousy, rape, xenophobia, and murder, but no biological explanation of those behaviors can be used to justify them in a moral sense. To use the culture concept to give a moral defense of any behavior is to commit the naturalistic fallacy in a new guise—call it the "culturalistic fallacy." No explanation of a behavior, whether it is based on biology, culture, or the phases of the moon, can ever be used to justify a behavior in moral terms.

If culture cannot be used to justify behavior, then perhaps we should get rid of cultural relativism entirely and replace it with something else, some approach to human affairs based on an absolute and universalistic moral code. For example, perhaps rather than just marveling at human diversity we should be social activists engaged in a moralistic quest to identify oppressors and oppressed, exploiters and exploited. This is what is advocated by, for example, Nancy Scheper-Hughes, an anthropologist at the University of California at Berkeley. Scheper-Hughes has shown how the poor of northeastern Brazil are kept poor and their children are kept sick and undernourished by a system involving physicians and the folk medical notion of a condition called "*nervos*." People who suffer from *nervos* may show a variety of symptoms including weakness, sleeplessness, headaches, and fainting. Scheper-Hughes argues that it is far from coincidental that these symptoms are the same one would expect from anyone who is chronically hungry. The solution offered by the Brazilian medical establishment is not food but tranquilizers, which make it doubly difficult for the people to do anything about their condition.[10] Other cultural practices around the world as troubling as the notion of *nervos* are not difficult to find. One that sometimes shocks Americans even more than female circumcision is the practice of hacking off little girls' fingers among the Dani of Irian Jaya, the western part of the island of New

Guinea. The practice is part of a particular Dani mourning ritual, and as a result of it some adult Dani women end up with only the thumb and two adjacent fingers of one hand remaining.[11]

People all over the political spectrum are bothered by the doctrine of cultural relativism in light of human rights abuses around the world. Recently Donald Hodel, a former Reagan administration official and now president of the Christian Coalition, a conservative, religious lobbying organization, argued in favor of a bill in Congress that would tie American foreign policy to religious freedom overseas. At a press conference where he lent the bill his group's support, Hodel argued that "this is an atrocity that's going on out there, and for people to suggest for a moment that well maybe we shouldn't be too concerned about somebody being hung upside down and beaten nearly to death and boiling oil poured over his feet . . . because maybe that's a cultural problem, I think is an abdication of our responsibility as free citizens of what ought to be a religiously safe world."[12]

Scheper-Hughes gets the moral code she applies to other societies from leftist political doctrines; Hodel gets his from the Judeo-Christian tradition and ideas about human rights developed during the Enlightenment. Still others propose a biological route around the problem of cultural relativism and toward a universal ethical system. Edward O. Wilson, for example, has recently argued that the naturalistic fallacy is no fallacy at all, and that, rather than rejecting evolutionary biology as a source of moral and ethical insights, we should be using it as the basis of a new and potentially universal ethical code. Ethical precepts, he writes, are not "ethereal messages outside humanity awaiting revelation" but rather "physical products of the brain and culture." Wilson argues that individuals are "predisposed biologically to make certain choices" about what is right and what is wrong that are then elevated through a process of cultural evolution to general principles. For example, here is the development he sees behind rules against adultery:

1. "Let's not go further; it doesn't feel right, it would lead to trouble."
2. "Adultery not only causes feelings of guilt, it is generally disapproved of by society, so these are other reasons to avoid it."
3. "Adultery isn't just disapproved of, it's against the law."
4. "God commands that we avoid this mortal sin."[13]

Does Wilson's "empirical" approach to ethics really let us escape from the problem of cultural relativism? What if someone with a somewhat different cultural background (say, a Mukogodo man) were faced with a similar concern with adultery? His ethical code might develop in quite a different way, such as this:

1. "Adultery is a problem. It destroys families and causes conflict in our society."
2. "One of the main reasons for adultery is women's pursuit of sexual pleasure."
3. "The clitoris is the main organ of sexual pleasure for most women."
4. "Therefore we should remove the clitorides of our women."
5. "Failure to remove the clitoris is shameful and dirty. No man should marry such an unclean woman."
6. "God wants us to perform clitoridectomies on all our women."

Although I certainly agree with Wilson that biology has much to teach us about the choices people make in life (see Chapter 4) and also that evolutionary biology has an important role to play in the empirical study of moral sentiments and systems (see Chapter 6), it is not clear that it is a sound basis on which to develop a system of ethics or that it truly offers us any way around the problem of cultural relativism.

Finding a Middle Ground

The very fact that, despite their common Western, Euro-American, Judeo-Christian cultural backgrounds, Scheper-Hughes, Hodel, and Wilson all come up with different sorts of absolutist moral codes suggests that there may be some life left in the old doctrine of cultural relativism after all. In defense of relativism, it is helpful to remember that our own behaviors are often just as disturbing to people with other cultural backgrounds as, say, female genital mutilation and the removal of little girls' fingers among the Dani are to us. This was brought home to me while I was among the Mukogodo. A teenage boy had heard from someone else that white people do not circumcise their girls and asked me whether it was true. When I told him that it was and then confirmed his logical conclusion that my own wife must not be circumcised, he came close to vomiting. To him, an uncircumcised woman is unclean, and certainly not to be married. Capital punishment is another custom that disturbs many people from other societies. Although it is popular among the American voting public, it is opposed as a human rights abuse by international human rights organizations and the governments of many other Western democracies. Clearly, some approach must be found that allows us to reap the benefits of cultural relativism while avoiding its pitfalls—to make moral judgments without assuming that ours is always the only "right" way of doing things.

I can offer three simple suggestions for how to reconcile our species' cultural diversity with our desire for a common, universal moral code. First, we need to stop thinking of cultures as coherent, integrated, bounded wholes and replace this with the idea that they are amorphous, unbounded bundles of ideas, knowledge, and beliefs that are continually being contested and renegotiated. Something close to this position has already become more or less the consensus among most cultural anthropologists, and it is in keeping with the approach to defining and using the culture concept described earlier in this book. This allows us to better understand the diversity that exists within cultures as well as between them; it also allows us to be less hesitant in judging the effects of culture traits. I can, for example, feel free to deplore the practice of female circumcision as a specific Mukogodo culture trait while simultaneously having deep respect for the rest of Mukogodo culture. I can love and respect my own American culture while opposing the death penalty. And so on.

Second, we need to keep in mind that culture traits are not and cannot be rights-bearing entities. The only things capable of having rights are people. This is one place where the viral analogy described in Chapter 5 is particularly useful. If culture traits are essentially like viruses, then clearly it makes no more sense to extend the protections of human rights to them than it would to extend them to, say, the smallpox virus. Students who defend the Holocaust and the judges who deny asylum to women avoiding circumcision on the grounds that such things are simply someone else's culture are, in effect, elevating the rights of culture traits above those of real, living people. The realization that culture is often a tool used by some people to manipulate others also helps us to see through the cloak that extreme relativism draws around it. If some cultural idea amounts to an attempt by some people to manipulate others, whether it is the concept of *nervos*, the doctrine of the divine right of kings, or the idea that those people who are different from us are somehow our enemies, then it is easy to see how protecting such a notion under the protective banner of cultural relativism can serve to perpetuate oppression and exploitation.

There is another, more defensible and legitimate argument for the preservation of cultural traits, but acting on it does not require violating anyone's rights. We may wish to preserve the many cultural traits that are rapidly disappearing from the world's societies for their potential usefulness in the future. Just as genetic diversity may be worth preserving because it may help the world deal with future biological crises, so we might be wise to keep a storehouse of the world's cultural knowledge in case it, too, can help us through hard times ahead. We are already beginning to recognize, for example, that we can learn a thing or two from traditional medical practices around the world, and it is likely that we would benefit from preserving and learning to appreciate many other sorts of folk knowledge and skills. Indeed, helping to preserve the world's cultural diversity, just as it is so rapidly disappearing, is one of the main ways in which anthropology can make itself useful. Fortunately for all concerned, doing so does not involve the violation of anyone's rights or forcing anyone to conform to traditional cultural traits that they no longer wish to follow.

Third, we need to foster the development of connections between the social sciences and the rest of the sciences. To reject all attempts to separate facts from values puts anthropologists and all other social scientists who deal with cultural difference on no firmer ground than religious missionaries, zealots with a passion not for understanding but for righting the wrongs of the world as they see them. As Roy D'Andrade of the University of California at San Diego has pointed out, we are more likely to have positive effects on the world if we first attempt to understand other societies before attempting to change them.[14] Understanding behavior across cultural gaps requires a sort of limited relativism that is no different from the usual detachment scientists show toward their subjects. Medical science is a good example of the power of this sort of attitude. Physicians, whose job it is to apply biological knowledge, have clear ideas about good and bad. Things that make people suffer, like viruses, are bad. Relieving people of problems caused by viruses and other pathogens is good. To achieve their goals, physicians must make use of knowledge gained by scientists about things like viruses. But it does not do any good for virologists to think of viruses as "bad" in some moralistic sense. They are simply fascinating and worthy of study in their own right. Similarly, it does the social scientist no good to make value judgments about the people, cultures, and societies he studies if his goal is simply to understand them. Such judgments may simply cloud his mind and make his primary tasks of explanation and understanding all the more difficult. Connecting the study of human affairs with the rest of the scientific project will help to foster an appropriate attitude of scientific detachment.

Sperm Banks and Shotgun Pellets

If a limited form of cultural relativism is worth salvaging from the wreckage of cultural determinism, another of its artifacts deserves to be jettisoned altogether: the treatment of culture as a political football. As we saw in Chapter 1, culture itself has become a hot political issue for the left and the right. These "culture wars" are based, fundamentally, on the idea that culture is such an overwhelmingly and uniquely powerful force in human affairs that it is worth waging a political struggle over it. If, as I have argued throughout this book, culture, though important, is by no means the only thing influencing human behavior, then we might do better as a society to try to appreciate and to concentrate on what we all share despite our various cultural exteriors and to focus our attention on more important sources of social problems.

It is not that William Bennett and others who would politicize culture don't have a point. Indeed, at the root of their discontent is something that I have also felt, something that has been increasingly felt by more and more people around the world. For most, it is simply a general malaise, a sense of unconnectedness, of not fitting in, a sense that we were not quite made for *this* world. And, of course, we weren't. We were made for a world that has mostly disappeared, a world in which we almost never dealt with strangers, in which an individual might see, let alone meet, just hundreds or at most thousands of other individuals in an entire lifetime, a world in which all activities were enmeshed in webs of kinship and friendship, a world in which things rarely changed much over the course of a lifetime. In contrast, when I stroll across the campus of my university during the few minutes between classes, I can see thousands of people, none of whom are my relatives, almost all of whom are complete strangers to me, all at an institution that, just in the time since I was born, has gone from a 2,000-student, virtually all white, all male, military school of agriculture and engineering to a well-rounded, coed, multiracial and multicultural university with 43,000 students. In many ways, it would be hard even for science fiction authors to dream up a world any more alien to the world in which humans evolved than the fast-changing, stranger-filled one in which we currently live. It is as if the dance between biology and culture has suddenly taken a nasty turn, with culture dancing to a fast, new tempo while biology continues its own steady waltz.

Consider, for instance, the following "help wanted" ad:

> Help wanted: Healthy males wanted as semen donors. Help infertile couples. Confidentiality ensured. Ages 18 to 35, excellent compensation.[15]

Here, one would think, is a perfect opportunity for young men to reproduce their genes. By the basic logic of natural selection, they should be flocking to sperm banks like the one that placed the advertisement, paying large sums of money and trying to look their best to be worthy of the chance to make a donation. But, of course, that is not how it works. Men are hardly knocking down sperm banks' doors for a chance to make a donation, despite the reproductive opportunity and good money that a frequent donor can make from literally a few minutes' work a week.

Observing people's glaring failure to take advantage of such an obvious opportunity for reproduction, a very naive student of natural selection might drop the whole theory like a hot potato. But a more sophisticated one would realize that evolution occurs to organisms in specific environments, and we can expect their adaptations to fit only those environments. If we take an organism out of the environment in which it evolved, or if its environment changes rapidly for some other reason, we have no reason to expect it to be able to cope adaptively with the new situation. British psychologist John Bowlby, in his seminal work *Attachment and Loss*, summed up this problem with the phrase "the environment of evolutionary adaptedness."[16] In an organism's environment of evolutionary adaptedness, we should be able to use the theory of natural selection to predict how it develops and behaves. Outside that environment, all bets are off. The psychology of human sexual attraction evolved in a world in which males' reproductive opportunities came in the form of human females, not petri dishes.

We humans are not the only ones who lately have found themselves in an unfamiliar world. Just as the growth of human populations, cities, and industrialism has altered our environment, so has it altered the environments of many animal species. Drivers in Texas are reminded of this almost daily by the carnage of armadillo carcasses on the state's highways. The armadillo's natural defense mechanism is to spring vertically into the air two or three feet. This must work well if the threat is a coyote, but it is not so good a defense against pick-up trucks. Many other animals have similar problems with highways and cars. Rabbits, for example, sometimes dart back and forth in the paths of oncoming cars, attempting to confuse what in their evolutionary past would have been a predator bearing down on them at high speed. Many other animals, like the feral hog I once killed with my Mazda, are notoriously bad at judging vehicles' speeds.

Toads have a different problem that stems from how they eat. A good amount of a normal toad lifetime is spent sitting around, eating small things that fly or crawl past its field of vision. In the environment of toad evolution, the only small things that flew or crawled were insects, so toads needed to make no more complex a judgment about what to eat than "is it small, and is it moving?" But bored American GIs in Korea found that they could kill time by rolling pellet after pellet past toads, watching them fill up like little amphibious beanbags. Toads were presented with another, similar problem when they were introduced to the Hawaiian islands in 1932. Some trees in those islands produce blossoms that are loaded with strychnine poison as a protection against insects, blossoms which blow off the trees and across the ground, where unsuspecting toads snatch them up. Shotgun pellets and poisonous flower blossoms acting like insects did not exist in the environment of toad evolution, and they had no reason to evolve any way to discriminate against them.[17]

We can begin to see the price we pay for living in our alien world with a look at modern health problems. It turns out that many of them, from various types of cancer to obesity to tooth decay to repetitive motion disorders, are the result of the mismatch between the way our ancestors lived and the way we do now. Obesity is an excellent example. How do we know what our palate has evolved to find tasty? All we can learn from the diets of the world's few remaining hunter-gatherer groups is what they find palatable given a restricted range of choices. To find out what people really like to eat, what they have evolved to like to eat, we need look no further than the local McDonald's, where the key ingredients are fat, salt, and sugar. In the environment of human evolution, these were relatively difficult things to get. Natural foods tend to be quite lean, not very sweet, and not very salty. In large amounts, all three are potential killers, but in small amounts they are excellent sources of calories and other nutrients, which, in naturally available foods, usually come packaged with a variety of nutrients in the form of animals, fruits, nuts, and vegetables. Even honey, which is little more than sugar and water, is traditionally eaten by the Mukogodo of Kenya and many other people together with the bee brood, a rich source of vitamin A. It made sense, then, for evolution to equip us with a strong yearning for these three basic things, because they were hard to get and worth spending some extra effort to find.

In the modern environment, though, fat, sugar, and salt are easy to find, and as a result many people have a terrible time keeping weight off, keeping their blood pressure, cholesterol, and triglyceride levels down, and fighting a daily battle against tooth decay. One person who can testify first hand to the problems of a modern diet and the benefits of an ancient one is Vaughn M. Bryant, Jr., head of my department at Texas A&M University. Bryant has spent much of his career using pollen, desiccated feces called coprolites, and other plant and animal remains to reconstruct the diets of people who lived thousands of years ago in the caves of Texas' Rio Grande valley. What he and his coworkers have found is that, in what must have been a difficult desert environment, the ancient Texans ate pretty much anything they could get their hands on, from small rodents swallowed whole to cactus pads, a diet rich in fiber and indigestible roughage and low in fat, sugar, and salt. Faced with health problems, Bryant designed his own high-fiber, low-fat, caveman diet, munching peanuts whole, including their shells, and gobbling up fruit, including cores, peels, seeds, and stems. Such a regime would not appeal to most people, but it is essentially what doctors recommend we all eat: less fat, sugar, and salt and more fiber and other roughage. In other words, we should be eating more of what our ancestors ate and less of what our tastebuds would like us to eat.[18]

We also should not be doing so much of what I am doing now (i.e., sitting at a computer, tapping at the keyboard and clicking a mouse for hour after hour). As so many office workers now know, this is a sure way to produce carpal tunnel syndrome and other potentially crippling repetitive motion disorders. Not very long ago, such repetitive activities were a rarity, partly because the division of labor was so much more simple. In a traditional farming community, for example, virtually everyone must do a wide variety of things just to make a living, from plowing and weeding to milking and cleaning stables. As the division of labor becomes more and more fine-grained, people find themselves doing more and more specialized tasks, often the same one for hour after hour, whether deboning chicken or soldering transistors onto circuit boards all day. In carpal tunnel syndrome, such repetitive actions inflame the tissues of the wrist and hand so that they press on the nerves that run through the carpal tunnel, causing pain, numbness, and weakness. Although assembly line workers have suffered from such ailments for years, the proliferation of computers has made the syndrome widespread. In some circles carpal tunnel syndrome is known as "computeritis" or "journalist's disease." In the words of Linda H. Morse, medical director of the Repetitive Motion Institute in San Jose, California, "the electronic revolution has outstripped our human muscular and skeletal evolution."

Most modern humans also suffer from far too little physical activity. My fingers may be busy as I write this, but using a keyboard is hardly an aerobic exercise. Many of us know that sedentism is a health problem and spend large amounts of money on exercise equipment and little-used memberships to health clubs. Our ancestors faced the opposite problem. Just making a living demanded plenty of exercise, and they did not need to take morning jogs on the savannah or steppe to stay in shape. Among the Mukogodo, most people are kept fit by herding and hauling water and firewood through the hills.

The prevalence of cancer in modern populations may also be a result of how different our environment is from that of our ancestors. Cancer is mostly a disease that strikes older people, and one reason why it seems to be much more common these days is simply because more people are living long enough—that is, *not* dying of the things that probably would have killed them in ages past—to die of cancer. In addition, some specific cancers—particularly breast cancer and cancers of the female reproductive system—seem to be made more common than they otherwise would be by certain aspects of our modern lives. A modern American woman typically has her first menses as early as age twelve, does not reproduce until she is at least in her twenties, and sometimes in her thirties or early forties, breastfeeds not at all or for only a short period, and experiences menopause in, say, her late 40s. Tampon manufacturers thrive because women who follow this pattern are rarely pregnant and rarely experience the suppression of the menstrual cycle that comes with steady breastfeeding, and thus experience a lot of cycles. This is not at all what women just a few generations ago experienced in Western society or what women experience in existing societies resembling those in which our ancestors lived. In those societies, menarche comes relatively late, usually after age 15, menopause comes relatively early, and for most of the time in between women are usually either pregnant or nursing, and thus not menstruating. This is true even of some women in our own society. While explaining why the Yanomamö pattern of squatting on the ground during a menstrual period is not such an inconvenience for women who rarely menstruate, Napoleon Chagnon recalls a time when his mother turned to him on a city bus and whispered, "My menstrual period is starting. This is the first one I've had in ten years." Though she lived in Michigan, Mrs. Chagnon followed a traditional reproductive pattern, bearing twelve children and breastfeeding each of them until they were about two years old.[19]

Such a way of life does have its health benefits. Studies have shown that breast cancer and cancers of the female reproductive system are reduced significantly if women get pregnant early, have several children, and breast-feed them for long periods. Breastfeeding's power to reduce the incidence of breast cancer can be most dramatically seen in a study among the Tanka, a fishing people in Hong Kong. Many Tanka women nurse their children with only the right breast, which is more convenient because their clothes open on the right. While breast cancer rates among older Tanka women in the right breast are quite low, in the other, unused breast they are equal to those found among modern American women.[20] In one study conducted on

American women by Peter M. Layde and his colleagues at the Centers for Disease Control, those who breast-fed for more than twenty-five months were 33 percent less likely to develop breast cancer than women who had children but had never breast-fed. Having more children helps, too, although it may require a large number of children for the effect to be measurable. Layde's study found that women with only one child had more than twice the cancer risk of women with seven or more children. A woman's reproductive history has similar effects on her chances of developing ovarian cancer and other cancers of the reproductive tract. At every age, there is a correlation between a woman's risk of developing a cancer of her reproductive tissues and the number of menstrual cycles she has experienced.[21]

Breastfeeding might also reduce the incidence of postpartum depression. Nursing stimulates a mother's production of a hormone called oxytocin, which has been shown to produce a warm, fuzzy feeling in humans and to encourage a variety of maternal behaviors in nonhuman mammals. Kelly Peyton, a recent product of my department's graduate program, has proposed that women who do not breast-feed may experience more postpartum depression than those who do because of their lack of oxytocin. Until very recently no mammalian mother, human or otherwise, would not breast-feed following a successful pregnancy, so the body of a woman who does not nurse her newborn is essentially receiving a signal of a failed pregnancy at precisely the same time that she is saddled with the responsibility of caring for a helpless, crying baby.[22]

Changes in what we eat, how we work, and how we reproduce are intimately connected to broader changes in our social lives, and it is those changes that may be at the root of the general malaise and sense of despair that plagues so many people in modern society. Sad to say, Theodore Kaczynski, the "Unabomber," may turn out to have been the defining figure of fin-de-siecle America. Kaczynski is at once one of the most glaring symptoms of the late twentieth century blues—an antisocial, alienated loner whose only way of interacting with the rest of society is to send death anonymously through the mail—and a surprisingly keen observer of the problem at hand. The "Unabomber's Manifesto," published in 1995 by the *Washington Post* and purportedly written by Kaczynski, describes the Industrial Revolution as "a disaster for the human race." Technology, he writes, has "made life unfulfilling" and has "led to widespread psychological suffering." Furthermore, he claims, the overwhelming demands of our society's moral code "can lead to low self-esteem, a sense of powerlessness, defeatism, guilt, etc." Because in "modern industrial society only minimal effort is necessary to satisfy one's physical needs" and all one needs to survive are "a moderate amount of intelligence, and, most of all, simple OBEDIENCE," people "become acutely bored and demoralized." What they need to be happy is a satisfying sequence of setting goals, striving for them, and attaining them, coupled with a sense of autonomy. Although "not all was sweetness and light in primitive societies," "primitive man suffered from less stress and frustration and was better satisfied with his way of life than modern man is."[23]

The Unabomber's account is not very different from what is coming to be known as "mismatch theory," the idea that many of our social and psychological problems arise from a mismatch between our ancestral and modern environments. David P. Barash, a professor of psychology and zoology at the University of Washington in Seattle, has argued that social pathologies such as drug use and crimes against strangers may reflect this mismatch. Although most traditional societies had a variety of drugs, they typically were not highly refined and required a lot of time and patience to acquire and prepare, so they rarely became the center of a person's life. Crime is less of a problem in such societies, or even in small towns in our society, because it is difficult to accomplish anonymously. "A small-town resident doesn't rob the corner grocery; everyone knows nice old Mr. McPherson," writes Barash. "But if McPherson is a nameless, familyless, disembodied, and anonymous spirit in a big city, he can be attacked with relative ease."[24] John Papworth, an Anglican priest, recently suggested that this sort of moral flexibility is understandable and even acceptable, remarking that "Jesus said, 'Love your neighbor,' he didn't say, 'Love Marks and Spencers.'" The Reverend Papworth continued, "If people wander in and wander out without paying for the stuff I think it is a perfectly comprehensible action."[25]

Tim Miller, a psychologist and author of a self-help book titled *How to Want What You Have: Discovering the Magic and Grandeur of Ordinary Existence* that incorporates some of the lessons of evolutionary psychology, argues that human nature equips us with desires for things that would have enhanced our ancestors' reproductive success, mainly wealth, status, and love. We strive to get them for the same reason we try to obtain fat, sugar, and salt: We are the descendants of those who were good at obtaining them in past environments. And, just as the modern environment allows us to overindulge our desires for fatty, sweet, and salty foods that turn out to be unhealthy and unsatisfying, so does it allow us to indulge our quest for wealth, status, and love, with an endless stream of new products, nearly limitless access to credit (and thus debt), and an ethic that, for many people, puts career advancement above practically all other goals. But an increasing number of people seem to be finding themselves on a treadmill, real happiness always just slightly out of reach.[26]

Although the first step to alleviating these sorts of problems of the modern condition is to understand them, none of the solutions will be easy or obvious. Breast cancer rates might be greatly reduced by a return to Paleolithic reproductive patterns, but to most people such a cure would be worse than the disease, in terms of how it would limit women's hard-won autonomy and in the population growth that would ensue. Once we have a better understanding of the details of the links between reproductive patterns and female cancers, a more probable solution would be to develop hormonal treatments that mimic the effects of our ancestors' reproductive habits of early and multiple pregnancies with long periods of breastfeeding in between. It may seem premature to consider such a drastic hormonal intervention into women's reproductive systems, but the recent changes in reproductive patterns have intervened in a way that is no less drastic, with no planning and no regard to possible side effects.

Solving the problem of the mismatch between the social environment of our ancestors and our own will undoubtedly be the most difficult of all these problems. Of course, the Unabomber has made one clear and simple suggestion, that we have a revolution to overthrow technology altogether, but the suffering caused by the modern condition would seem tiny in comparison with that produced by such a change. As problematic as technology, a complex division of labor, and the rest of the modern industrial system may be, there is no avoiding that in many ways they make happiness easier rather than more difficult for many people to achieve. We can, after all, be confident that our children will survive to adulthood, and we can choose our mates and our occupations and even how to spend our spare time, luxuries unavailable to most of our ancestors. Whatever solutions are offered must not come at the expense of our health or our newfound freedoms.

When Things Were *Really* Rotten

As problematic as modern society may be for organisms like us who evolved to deal with a different environment, it could be worse. Indeed, not long ago it *was* worse for quite a lot of the world's population. This is because, in many ways, the societies that are most unlike those in which we evolved are not modern, industrialized ones but, rather, the sort of rigid, hierarchical, and politically oppressive ones that sprung up after the development of agriculture like mushrooms after a rain. I am thinking in particular of the more elaborate chiefdoms and early state societies that first developed in places like Mesopotamia and the Nile Valley but that are better documented in places where they developed more recently such as the Americas, parts of Africa, and Polynesia. Admittedly, most available accounts of these sorts of societies were written by opinionated and often unfriendly folks with their own religious, political, and economic agendas, and so need to be taken with a grain of salt or two. However, the picture they paint is a consistently and painfully bleak one. These complex chiefdoms and early states appear to be have been remarkably nasty places, rife with torture, arbitrary killing, and religious doctrines that were designed to maintain the positions of the elites, sometimes even requiring human sacrifices. Rigid caste systems and onerously heavy taxation were routine. Typically, the status of women also dropped as the patriarchal state became a new tool for their oppression.

The extreme nastiness of such societies probably had a lot to do with their own novelty. Everything about them was new, including not only the differentiation of people into different social classes with different rights, privileges, and amounts of wealth but even the idea of the "state" and its central monopoly on the use of force. In earlier societies, as in contemporary band and tribal societies, everyone had the right to use force as they saw fit. No one had the right to push anyone else around. But states involve the centralization of the right to use force, and making that concentration of force seem legitimate and right—or at least unchangeable—to the bulk of the population seems to have been a major worry of early state rulers. Ideology played its part in crowd control, with notions such as the divinity of the king being invented independently in several different times and places, but the basic tools of elite domination were often much more simple: violence and the threat of violence. Consider, for instance, the kingdom of Buganda in what is now Uganda. Buganda was a centralized, bureaucratic state ruled by an autocratic king known as the kabaka. It was similar to a series of other kingdoms around East Africa's great lakes, including Bunyoro, Ankole, Rwanda, and Burundi. Buganda's kabakas had an enormous amount of arbitrary power over the life and death of their subjects and, before the arrival of Islamic and Christian missionaries in the nineteenth century, their word was absolute law. If the kabaka decided, on the advice of a fortune teller, that everyone in the kingdom with cataracts should be put to death, it was done. When the kabaka Mwanga's rule was threatened in the late nineteenth century by conversions to Christianity, his response was swift and simple: the murders of two hundred Protestant and Catholic converts.[27] Similar stories are told of despots from many similar societies. Tanoa, a nineteenth-century king of

Fiji, for example, is said to have killed and cannibalized slaves and maybe other subjects with no provocation.[28]

In comparison to such terror-filled, hierarchical, oppressive societies, our society bears some surprising similarities to those in which we evolved. As the power of despots has declined and the power of average citizens has risen, we have managed, mostly without planning, to recreate some of the practices and social patterns that are typical of simple, hunting and gathering band societies. For instance, while there is no arguing that our society is divided into social classes, it is much more egalitarian in ideology and in reality than were the rigid hierarchical societies of the not too distant past. This relative egalitarianism has many aspects. Economically, there is a great deal more movement among socioeconomic classes in our society than in most historically recorded ones. Politically, the expansion of suffrage over the past couple of centuries has done much to open the government to participation by many groups who were previously excluded, including the landless, religious and racial minorities, and women. Socially, modern societies take seriously the idea that we all should be maritally equal. In contrast to many historical societies, where men in the upper classes, especially rulers, typically had more wives and concubines than average men, in our society the rule of one spouse per person at a time is taken seriously. Sexually, although we still have a long way to go in creating a society without gender biases, it is safe to say that a person's gender has much less to do with his or her occupation or status in society than it has in almost all previous human societies. In terms of religion and ideology, we are a long way from the mandatory adherence to official dogma that characterized earlier state societies. Rather, we are free to believe and worship as we wish. Increasingly, phenomena such as the New Age movement have opened the door to personal spiritual experimentation, with each individual being encouraged to find his or her own mix of beliefs and practices with few worries about any form of orthodoxy.

These patterns are not that different from those found in band societies. In bands, there is no measurable "wealth," there are no social classes or heritable differences in status or prestige, and everyone has an equal voice in group activities. Typically in band societies, although men and women may have different economic roles, their status is roughly equal. Although polygyny and polyandry are usually permitted and occasionally found in band societies, monogamy is the norm for almost everyone. And the sort of individualized religion that is becoming so popular in our society bears some resemblance to the freedom people in band societies have been observed to have concerning precisely what to believe and how to worship.

In other ways, modern society actually makes good, constructive use of our evolved human nature. Adoption of the babies of strangers, for instance, is virtually unheard of in most traditional societies. In large part, this is simply because people in such societies almost never interact with strangers. Adoption does occur in traditional societies, but it almost always involves nieces, nephews, and other relatives. Our mass society, on the other hand, allows us to take advantage of the desire so many people have to nurture and care for babies and children by connecting them with children whose own parents are not in a position to provide such care. Perhaps this sort of creative coupling of our evolved psychological propensities with cultural innovations that are possible only in a mass society such as ours will provide a way to build a new society that retains the best features of our ancestors' worlds and our own.

Lonesome No More?

It may be possible to try to mimic, in small ways at least, aspects of the environment of human evolutionary adaptedness that might help make this world seem less alien and more familiar. Our ancestors lived their entire lives in the nexus of kinship, with families, kindreds, and lineages providing economic aid, child care, help in finding mates, emotional support, and a variety of other types of assistance. In his novel *Slapstick*, Kurt Vonnegut noted the alienation of modern society and offered a suggestion for how to solve it.[29] The subtitle of the book, *Lonesome No More!*, refers to the campaign slogan of Wilbur Daffodil–11 Swain, the last president of the United States. His sole issue is the loneliness of his compatriots, and his solution is to use the computers of the federal government to recreate kinship networks like those of our ancestors. In this fantasy, everyone gets a new middle name corresponding to something in nature—Chipmunk, Hollyhock, Raspberry, Uranium—and a number. By name and number everyone is instantly related to 10,000 brothers and sisters and 190,000 cousins, all obligated to help fellow clan members. That is a lot of kin, but, as Swain observes, "We need all the help we can get in a country as big and clumsy as ours."[30]

Closer to reality, my institution, Texas A&M University, has done an admirable job of keeping a small-scale feel at the same time that it has exploded in enrollment. This was accomplished through a deliberate policy of indoctrinating students into what it means to be an Aggie, as A&M students are called. The socialization process begins during the summer before the freshmen (or "fish," as they are called here) arrive at "Fish Camp," where upperclassmen teach the new students the university's folklore and its many traditions. This creates a strong feeling of shared identity and common purpose, and helps to make an institution with 43,000 students feel a great deal smaller and more personal than most big state universities while still tolerant and open to diversity (drawing the line, perhaps, at incursions from the rival University of Texas at Austin). One of the Aggie traditions is simply saying the word "howdy" to virtually anyone one might pass on campus. It may sound contrived, but receiving greetings from strangers just walking across campus creates a real sense of friendliness and openness that I honestly miss when I visit other universities and large cities, where eye contact with strangers is avoided at almost all costs. I see no reason why a variety of institutions, not just universities but corporations and other bureaucracies, could not adopt similar policies of encouraging behaviors that make friendliness and sociability routine and give people a feeling of belonging to an inclusive, supportive social network.

In the long run, perhaps we will evolve to fit our new environment. We may feel less need for supportive networks of kin and friends, our bodies may come to cope with the abundance of fat in our environment, and, as sperm banks account for more and more babies, men may even evolve a propensity to find test tubes downright arousing. Men like Cecil B. Jacobson, a Fairfax, Virginia infertility specialist who, unbeknownst to the women involved, used his own sperm to sire perhaps as many as seventy children, may be the fathers of the future (he certainly is leaving many more copies of his genes behind than most of us).[31] But, surely, it will be a long time before laboratory supply catalogs are sold from behind the counter at convenience stores, and before armadillos stop littering Texas highways. In the meantime, we must strive for ways to live peacefully and happily with one another, products of the Stone Age living in an all too modern world.

Notes

Preface

1. Wilson 1975, Dawkins 1976.
2. Sahlins 1976.
3. Pinker 1994.
4. de Waal 1996, B1.
5. Dawkins 1995, 31.
6. Tiger 1996, 25.
7. Cronk in press, b.
8. Cronk 1992.

Chapter 1

1. Bennett 1992, 195.
2. Bennett 1992, 258.
3. Bennett 1992, 35.
4. Bennett 1993, 1995a, 1995b.
5. These biographical details about E. B. Tylor are taken from Moore 1997.
6. Tylor 1871, 1.
7. This label is attributed to Max Müller, a religious scholar (Moore 1997, 17).
8. Table 1.1 (see below) summarizes the definitions of culture given in the textbooks.
9. Nozick 1974, 19.
10. Mills 1940, 329.
11. See Cronk 1989b, Cronk 1993, and Cronk in press a.
12. See Cronk 1991a, Cronk 1991b, and Cronk in press a.
13. The exclamation point represents one of the many click sounds used in the !Kung language as well as in some other languages from southern and eastern Africa. Specifically, it represents what linguists call an alveopalatal click. To make it, press your tongue against the roof of your mouth and then pull it away sharply.
14. On the Herero, see Harpending and Pennington 1993; on Ifaluk, see Betzig and Turke 1986.
15. Hrdy 1990, Brauchli 1991.
16. Deutscher (1973) and Deutscher, Pestello, and Pestello (1993) are two useful

Table 1.1   Definitions of culture given in anthropology textbooks

Definition	*Source*
The patterned and learned ways of life and thought shared by a human society.	Bodley 1994:7
The capacity to use tools and symbols.	Bohannan 1992:320
A learned system of beliefs, feelings, and rules for living around which a group of people organize their lives; a way of life of a particular society.	Crapo 1996:17
The learned set of behaviors, beliefs, attitudes, values, or ideals that are characteristic of a particular society or population.	Ember and Ember 1990:357
Everything that people have, think, and do as members of a society.	Ferraro, Trevathan, and Levy 1994:18
The behavior, ideas, and institutions that are acquired by people as members of a society.	Gross 1992:15
The learned patterns of behavior and thought characteristic of a societal group.	Harris 1993:482
A set of rules or standards shared by members of a society, which when acted upon by the members produce behavior that falls within a range of variation the members consider proper and acceptable.	Haviland 1996:32
Everything that people collectively do, think, make, and say.	Hicks and Gwynne 1994:391
The customary manner in which human groups learn to organize their behavior in relation to their environment.	Howard and Dunaif-Hattis 1992:622
Traditions and customs, transmitted through learning, that govern the beliefs and behavior of the people exposed to them.	Kottak 1994:2
That complex of behavior and beliefs we learn from being members of our group.	Moore 1992:11
The learned behaviors and symbols that allow people to live in groups, the primary means by which humans adapt to their environments. The way of life characteristic of a particular human society.	Nanda and Warms 1998:381

(continues)

Definition	Source
The socially transmitted knowledge and behavior shared by some group of people.	Peoples and Bailey 1997:412
The system of meanings about the nature of experience that are shared by a people and passsed on from one generation to another.	Robbins 1997:229
The way of life of a people, including their behavior, the things they make, and their ideas.	Rosman and Rubel 1998:372
Sets of learned behavior and ideas that human beings acquire as members of society.	Schultz and Lavenda 1995:5
A shared way of life that includes material products, values, beliefs, and norms that are transmitted within a particular society from generation to generation.	Scupin 1992:414
A way of life that is common to a group of people, including a collection of beliefs and attitudes, shared understandings, and patterns of behavior that allow those people to live together in relative harmony, but set them apart from other peoples.	Whiteford and Friedl 1992:80
According to E. B. Taylor, "The complex whole which includes knowledge, belief, art, law, morals, custom and any other capabilities and habits acquired by man as a member of society."	Womack 1998: 420

sources and critiques of sociological and social psychological literature on discrepancies between statements and behavior.

17. LaPiere 1934.

18. Lohman and Reitzes 1954.

19. DeFleur and Westie 1958.

20. Warriner 1958.

21. Liebow 1967.

22. Cancian 1975.

23. Hrdy 1990.

24. D'Andrade 1992, 23.

25. Kroeber and Kluckhohn 1952, 155.

26. See Keesing (1974) for a good description of the development of an ideational definition of culture.

27. Geertz 1973.

28. Dan Sperber (1985) has said essentially the same thing about the material nature of culture.

29. Dawkins 1976.

30. For two mathematically sophisticated treatments of memetic transmission and evolution, see Cavalli-Sforza and Feldman 1982 and Boyd and Richerson 1985.

31. On animal cultures, see Bonner 1980, McGrew 1992, and Wrangham et al., eds., 1994.

Chapter 2

1. Eddington 1928, 266–67.

2. Fisher 1930, ix.

3. Le Guin 1969.

4. Kroeber 1961.

5. Mead 1928.

6. Coolidge 1921, 14.

7. Freeman 1989.

8. Mead 1935.

9. See Gewertz 1981.

10. This misunderstanding is attributable to Benjamin Whorf (see Carroll 1956).

11. See Malotki 1983.

12. Ekman 1972, 1973.

13. Maintained by Human Relations Area Files, Inc., of New Haven, Connecticut. Most large research university libraries have a copy.

14. Murdock 1967.

15. Schusky 1983.

16. Brown 1991.

17. Brown 1991, 130–141.

18. Dressler 1989.

19. Sawyer and Levine 1966.

20. Williams 1992, Chapter 6.

21. Borgerhoff Mulder 1989.

22. T. J. McMillan, personal conversation, 17 November 1989.

23. Cronk 1989a.

24. Tiger and Shepher 1975; van den Berghe 1979, 70–74.

25. Mandelker 1984.

26. Fuller 1976.

27. Ingold 1994, 22.

28. This "jukebox behavior" example is borrowed from Tooby and Cosmides 1992, 115–116.

29. McFarland Symington 1987.

30. Thornhill 1981.

31. Davies 1992.

32. Woolfenden and Fitzpatrick 1984.
33. Quoted in Heimans 1988.
34. Cronk 1989c.
35. See Cherfas and Gribbin 1984.

Chapter 3

1. Liebig 1842, 1.
2. Lowie [1917] 1929, 66.
3. Russell 1969, 9.
4. Wilson 1975.
5. Rosenberg 1980, x.
6. Freeman 1982. See also Caton, ed., 1990 and Freeman 1998.
7. Gonzalez 1984.
8. Freeman 1989, Heimans 1988.
9. Popper 1978, 33–39.
10. Darwin [1872] 1958, 186.
11. Hayek 1955, see also Aberle 1987.
12. Kuhn 1962.
13. Harpending 1995, 100.
14. This idea, and indeed much of this chapter, owes a lot to Tooby and Cosmides 1992.
15. On emergence, see Weinberg 1992 and Kauffman 1995.
16. Carl Menger (1892) is the original source of this classic account of the origins of money. On the broader topic of spontaneous social orders, see Cronk 1988 and the references cited therein, particularly those by Carl Menger and F. A. Hayek.
17. Dawkins 1976.
18. Lowie [1917] 1929, 66.
19. Durkheim 1938.
20. Quoted from a first draft of Rosaldo (1984) by Spiro (1984).
21. Peacock 1986.
22. Marcus and Fischer 1986, 43.
23. Tooby and Cosmides 1992, 19.
24. Aunger 1995.
25. Key works in the textualist or postmodernist critique of ethnography include Clifford and Marcus, eds., 1986, Clifford 1988, Crapanzano 1980, Geertz 1988, Marcus and Cushman 1982, and Marcus and Fischer 1986. Some of the responses to this critique can be found in Aunger 1995; Bailey 1991; Carrithers 1990; Cronk 1998; Kuper 1992; Kuznar 1997; O'Meara 1989, 1997; and Reyna 1994.
26. A good starting point for anyone interested in archaeological site formation processes is Schiffer 1987.
27. For a more detailed presentation of the argument in this section, see Cronk 1998.

28. For examples of this trend, see Sanjek, ed., 1990, and Wolf 1992.

29. Silverman 1972.

30. Wilson 1998.

31. I have borrowed this example from Cosmides, Tooby, and Barkow 1992, 13–14. For more on the debate over the age of the Earth, see Albritton 1980 and Dalrymple 1991.

Chapter 4

1. Classified advertisements from the *Austin American-Statesman* for March 6, 1997 and December 5, 1996, respectively.

2. Several good and accessible accounts of this new approach to human behavior have been published in recent years. See, for example, Allman 1994; Pinker 1997; Ridley 1993, 1996; and Wright 1994.

3. Wynne-Edwards 1962.

4. Key neofunctionalist works include Harris 1966, 1979; Rappaport 1968; and Vayda et al. 1961.

5. Rappaport 1968.

6. Rappaport 1968, 195.

7. Wynne-Edwards 1962, 16.

8. Rappaport 1994, 331.

9. Williams 1966.

10. Although the idea that group selection is likely to be important to an understanding of the evolution of behavior remains a minority position among evolutionary biologists, it does have its champions. For a recent attempt to apply a group selectionist model to the study of humans, see Wilson and Sober 1994.

11. For some excellent work on elephant seals, see Le Boeuf 1974.

12. Ellis and Symons 1990.

13. Townsend 1989, 1993; Townsend and Levy 1990a, 1990b.

14. Deaux and Hanna 1984, Greenlees and McGrew 1994, Thiessen et al. 1993, Wiederman 1993.

15. Buss et al. 1990, Buss 1994.

16. Borgerhoff Mulder 1988, 1990.

17. Hamilton 1964.

18. Sherman 1977.

19. Emlen and Wrege 1988.

20. Packer et al. 1991.

21. Chagnon and Bugos 1979.

22. Daly and Wilson 1988.

23. Sahlins 1976, 18.

24. Sahlins 1976, 26.

25. Hawkes 1983.

26. Blurton Jones, Marlowe, Hawkes, and O'Connell in press; Hawkes 1990,

1991, 1993; Hawkes, Hill, and O'Connell 1982; Hawkes and O'Connell 1983; Hawkes, O'Connell, and Blurton Jones 1989; and Hawkes, O'Connell, Blurton Jones, Alvarez, and Charnov in press.

27. Mayr 1961, Tinbergen 1963.

28. See, for example, Hepper, ed., 1991.

29. Blurton Jones 1987, Konner and Worthman 1980.

Chapter 5

1. Lang 1997.

2. Irons 1997.

3. Irons 1979.

4. Cronk 1991c.

5. Hill and Kaplan 1988a, 1988b; Kaplan and Hill 1985.

6. Chagnon 1988a; Chagnon 1979.

7. Moore 1990.

8. Cronk 1989a.

9. Turke 1989.

10. Pérusse 1993.

11. See, for example, Bloom 1995, Brodie 1995, Dennett 1995, Lumsden and Wilson 1982, and Lynch 1996. For more technical treatments of this subject see Barkow 1989, Boyd and Richerson 1985, Cavalli-Sforza and Feldman 1981, Durham 1991, Lumsden and Wilson 1981, and Pulliam and Dunford 1980.

12. But it is quite possible for such memes to enhance the reproductive success of their bearers. Stark (1996) has presented evidence that members of the early Christian church had higher fertility and lower mortality than the pagans in the Roman Empire at the time, and the more recent case of high reproductive rates among Mormons is already widely known.

13. Dawkins 1976, 205.

14. This account of *kuru* among the Fore is borrowed from Durham 1991, Chapter 7.

15. Although the brain of an adult human accounts for only about two percent of body weight, it requires twenty percent of the body's metabolic energy (Rosenzweig 1979, 291).

16. Boyd and Richerson 1985, Chapter 7.

17. Soltis, Boyd, and Richerson 1995.

18. See Cronk 1994a, 1994b, and 1995 for more on the arguments made in this chapter and the next one.

Chapter 6

1. Dawkins and Krebs 1978, 282.

2. Bailey 1991, xv.

3. I am indebted to Peter J. Richerson for pointing this out to me.

4. Harpending, Rogers, and Draper 1987.

5. Humphrey 1976, reprinted in Byrne and Whiten, eds., 1988.

6. Jolly 1966, Premack and Woodruff 1978, and the papers collected in Byrne and Whiten, eds., 1988.

7. Cosmides 1989, Cosmides and Tooby 1992.

8. Alexander 1987.

9. More or less this same idea has been invented separately by economist Robert H. Frank (1988) and animal behaviorist Amotz Zahavi (Zahavi et al. 1997). The college degree example comes from Frank, while the lace example comes from Zahavi.

10. Seuss 1961.

11. Alexander 1975; see also Bailey 1991.

12. Dawkins and Guilford 1991.

13. Dunbar 1996; for an excellent discussion of the evolutionary biological study of the origins of language, see Pinker 1994.

14. Chagnon 1988b, in press.

15. Daly and Wilson 1983; Johnson 1986, 1987, and 1989; Salmon 1998.

16. Harpending, Rogers, and Draper 1987.

17. Caldwell et al. 1988.

18. Vlassoff and Vlassoff 1980.

19. Cronk 1990, 1994a.

20. Crissman et al. 1989.

21. Chagnon 1974, 1997.

22. Scott 1985, 1990.

23. Scott 1990.

24. See Aunger 1994 for an example of this sort of experiment.

25. Read 1965.

Chapter 7

1. Barkow 1989, 373.

2. See Kassindja et al. 1998 for more details on this story.

3. Boas 1940, 60–75.

4. On June 23, 1993 in Prince William County, Virginia, Lorena Bobbitt sliced off her husband John's penis while he slept. Unlike the clitorides of women who experience clitoridectomies, John Bobbitt's penis was recovered and surgically reattached.

5. The nineteenth-century British physician Isaac Baker Brown was a prominent advocate of clitoridectomies to treat such symptoms of "uterine madness" and nymphomania as masturbation, though he was eventually expelled from the Obstetrical Society of London for coercing patients into accepting the treatment (Moscucci 1990, 105; see also Dedman 1991).

6. Judgment made on April 28, 1995 in the case of an asylum applicant referred to as "D.J."

7. Judgment made August 9, 1995 in the case of an asylum applicant from Sierra Leone.

8. Hume 1739/40.

9. Moore 1903, 10.

10. Scheper-Hughes 1992, 1995.

11. Heider 1991.

12. Quoted in a story reported by Lynn Neary on the National Public Radio program *All Things Considered* aired August 26, 1997.

13. Wilson 1998, 250.

14. D'Andrade 1995.

15. At one time this advertisement ran every day in *The Battalion*, Texas A&M University's campus newspaper.

16. Bowlby 1969.

17. My thanks to herpetologist James R. Dixon, Professor Emeritus in the Department of Wildlife and Fisheries Sciences at Texas A&M University, for this information about toads.

18. Bryant 1979, 1994, 1995. See also Eaton, Shostak, and Konner 1988.

19. Chagnon 1992, 152.

20. Ing, Petrakis, and Ho 1977.

21. Layde et al. 1989.

22. Peyton 1996.

23. Kaczynski's "Unabomber Manifesto" is available on the World Wide Web: http://www.panix.com/~clays/Una/index.html

24. Barash 1986.

25. Quoted in an article in *The Eagle*, Bryan-College Station, Texas, March 16, 1997, pp. A1, A6.

26. Miller 1995. See also Barkow 1997.

27. On Buganda, see Kagwa 1934, Roscoe 1911, and Speke 1864.

28. Williams 1884. For an evolutionary biological analysis of the behavior of despots like Mwanga and Tanoa, see Betzig 1986.

29. Vonnegut 1976.

30. A considerably more serious and promising approach has been taken to this problem by University of Nebraska psychologist Mary Pipher (1996).

31. Sforza 1995.

References

Aberle, David F. 1987. "Distinguished Lecture: What Kind of Science Is Anthropology?" *American Anthropologist* 89 (3):551–566.

Albritton, Claude C., Jr. 1980. *The Abyss of Time*. San Francisco: Freeman, Cooper.

Alexander, Richard. 1975. "The Search for a General Theory of Behavior." *Behavioral Science* 20:77–100.

———. 1987. *The Biology of Moral Systems*. Hawthorne, NY: Aldine de Gruyter.

Allman, William F. 1994. *The Stone Age Present*. New York: Simon & Schuster.

Aunger, Robert. 1994. "Sources of Variation in Ethnographic Interview Data: Food Avoidances in the Ituri Forest, Zaire." *Ethnology* 33:65–99.

———. 1995. "On Ethnography: Storytelling or Science?" *Current Anthropology* 36 (1):97–130.

Bailey, F. G. 1991. *The Prevalence of Deceit*. Ithaca: Cornell University Press.

Barash, David. 1986. *The Hare and the Tortoise: Culture, Biology, and Human Nature*. New York: Viking.

Barkow, Jerome H. 1989. *Darwin, Sex, and Status*. Toronto, ON: University of Toronto Press.

———. 1997. "Happiness in Evolutionary Perspective." In *Uniting Psychology and Biology: Integrative Perspectives on Human Development*. Nancy L. Segal, Glenn E. Weisfeld, and Carol C. Weisfeld, eds. Washington, D.C.: American Psychological Association.

Bennett, William J. 1992. *The De-Valuing of America: The Fight for Our Culture and Our Children*. New York: Summit.

———. 1993. *The Book of Virtues*. New York: Simon & Schuster.

———. 1995a. *The Children's Book of Virtues*. New York: Simon & Schuster.

———. 1995b. *Moral Compass*. New York: Simon & Schuster.

Betzig, Laura L. 1986. *Despotism and Differential Reproduction: A Darwinian View of History*. New York: Aldine de Gruyter.

Betzig, Laura L., and Paul Turke. 1986. "Parental Investment by Sex on Ifaluk." *Ethology and Sociobiology* 7:29–37.

Bloom, Howard K. 1995. *The Lucifer Principle*. New York: The Atlantic Monthly Press.

Blurton Jones, Nicholas G. 1987. "Bushman Birth Spacing: Direct Tests of Some Simple Predictions." *Ethology and Sociobiology* 8:183–204.

Blurton Jones, Nicholas G., Frank W. Marlowe, Kristen Hawkes, and James F. O'Connell. In press. "Hunter-Gatherer Divorce Rates and the Paternal Investment Theory of Human Pair-Bonding." In *Adaptation and Human Behavior: An Anthropological Perspective*. L. Cronk, N. Chagnon, and W. Irons, eds. Hawthorne, NY: Aldine de Gruyter.

Boas, Franz. 1940. *Race, Language, and Culture*. New York: Macmillan.

Bodley, John H. 1994. *Cultural Anthropology: Tribes, States, and the Global System*. Mountain View, CA: Mayfield.

Bohannan, Paul. 1992. *We, the Alien*. Prospect Heights, IL: Waveland.

Bonner, John Tyler. 1980. *The Evolution of Culture in Animals*. Princeton: Princeton University Press.

Borgerhoff Mulder, Monique. 1988. "Kipsigis Bridewealth Payments." In *Human Reproductive Behaviour: A Darwinian Perspective*. L. Betzig, M. Borgerhoff Mulder, and Paul Turke, eds. Cambridge: Cambridge University Press.

———. 1989. "Reproductive Consequences of Sex-Biased Inheritance." In *Comparative Socioecology of Mammals and Man*. V. Standen and R. A. Foley, eds. London: Blackwell Scientific.

———. 1990. "Kipsigis Women's Preferences for Wealthy Men: Evidence for Female Choice in Mammals?" *Behavioral Ecology and Sociobiology* 27:255–264.

Bowlby, John. 1969. *Attachment and Loss*. New York: Basic.

Boyd, Robert, and Peter J. Richerson. 1985. *Culture and the Evolutionary Process*. Chicago: University of Chicago Press.

Brauchli, Marcus W. 1991. "Garment Industry Booms in Bangladesh: Factory Jobs for Women Change Lives for Many." *Wall Street Journal*, August 6. p. A13.

Brodie, Richard. 1995. *Virus of the Mind*. Seattle: Integral.

Brown, Donald E. 1991. *Human Universals*. New York: McGraw-Hill.

Bryant, Vaughn M., Jr. 1979. "I Put Myself on a Caveman Diet—Permanently." *Prevention* 31 (9):128–137.

———. 1994. "The Paleolithic Health Club." In *1995 Yearbook of Science and the Future*. David Calhoun, ed. Chicago: Encyclopedia Britannica.

———. 1995. "Eating Right Is an Ancient Rite." *The World & I* 10 (1):216–221.

Buss, David M. 1994. *The Evolution of Desire: Strategies of Human Mating*. New York: Basic.

Buss, David M. et al. 1990. "International Preferences in Selecting Mates: A Study of 37 Cultures." *Journal of Cross-Cultural Psychology* 21:5–47.

Byrne, Richard, and Andrew Whiten, eds. 1988. *Machiavellian Intelligence*. Oxford: Clarendon.

Caldwell, J. C., P. H. Reddy, and P. Caldwell. 1988. *The Causes of Demographic Change*. Madison: University of Wisconsin Press.

Cancian, Francesca M. 1975. *What are Norms?: A Study of Beliefs and Action in a Maya Community*. London and New York: Cambridge University Press.

Carrithers, Michael. 1990. "Is Anthropology Art or Science?" *Current Anthropology* 31(3):263–282.

Carroll, John B., ed. 1956. *Language, Thought, and Reality: Selected Writings of Benjamin Lee Whorf.* Boston: Technology Press of MIT.

Caton, Hiram, ed. 1990. *The Samoa Reader: Anthropologists Take Stock.* Lanham, MD: University Press of America.

Cavalli-Sforza, Luigi Luca, and Marcus W. Feldman. 1982. *Cultural Transmission and Evolution.* Princeton: Princeton University Press.

Chagnon, Napoleon A. 1974. *Studying the Yanomamö.* New York: Holt, Rinehart, and Winston.

———. 1979. "Is Reproductive Success Equal in Egalitarian Societies?" In *Evolutionary Biology and Human Social Behavior: An Anthropological Perspective.* N. A. Chagnon and W. Irons, eds. North Scituate, MA: Duxbury.

———. 1988a. "Life Histories, Blood Revenge, and Warfare in a Tribal Population." *Science* 238:985–992.

———. 1988b. "Male Yanomamö Manipulations of Kinship Classifications of Female Kin for Reproductive Advantage." In *Human Reproductive Behaviour: A Darwinian Perspective.* L. Betzig, M. Borgerhoff Mulder, and Paul Turke, eds. Cambridge: Cambridge University Press.

———. 1992. *Yanomamö: The Last Days of Eden.* San Diego: Harcourt Brace Jovanovich.

———. 1997. *Yanomamö.* 5th ed. Fort Worth: Harcourt Brace College Publishers.

———. In press. "Adult Yanomamö Classification Accuracy for First Ascending Generation Kin." In *Adaptation and Human Behavior: An Anthropological Perspective.* L. Cronk, N. A. Chagnon, and W. Irons, eds. Hawthorne, NY: Aldine de Gruyter.

Chagnon, Napoleon A., and Paul E. Bugos, Jr. 1979. "Kin Selection and Conflict: An Analysis of a Yanomamö Ax Fight." In *Evolutionary Biology and Human Social Behavior: An Anthropological Perspective.* N. A. Chagnon and W. Irons, eds. North Scituate, MA: Duxbury.

Cherfas, Jeremy, and John Gribbin. 1984. *The Redundant Male: Is Sex Irrelevant in the Modern World?* New York: Pantheon.

Clifford, James. 1988. *The Predicament of Culture.* Cambridge: Harvard University Press.

Clifford, James, and George E. Marcus. 1986. *Writing Culture: The Poetics and Politics of Ethnography.* Berkeley: University of California Press.

Coolidge, Calvin. 1921. "Whose Country Is This?" *Good Housekeeping* 72:13–14, 106, 109.

Cosmides, Leda. 1989. "The Logic of Social Exchange: Has Natural Selection Shaped How Humans Reason?" *Cognition* 31:187–276.

Cosmides, Leda, and John Tooby. 1992. "Cognitive Adaptations for Social Exchange." In *The Adapted Mind: Evolutionary Psychology and the Generation of Cul-*

ture. Jerome H. Barkow, Leda Cosmides, and John Tooby, eds. Oxford: Oxford University Press.

Cosmides, Leda, John Tooby, and Jerome H. Barkow. 1992. "Introduction: Evolutionary Psychology and Conceptual Integration." In *The Adapted Mind: Evolutionary Psychology and the Generation of Culture.* Jerome H. Barkow, Leda Cosmides, and John Tooby, eds. Oxford: Oxford University Press.

Crapanzano, Vincent. 1980. *Tuhami: Portrait of a Moroccan.* Chicago: University of Chicago Press.

Crapo, Richard H. 1996. *Cultural Anthropology: Understanding Ourselves and Others.* Madison, WI: Brown and Benchmark.

Crissman, J. K., J. F. Iaccino, and T. G. Jelen. 1989. "The Relationship of Aging to Perceptions of the Performance of Household Chores." *Journal of Social Behavior and Personality* 4:471–480.

Cronk, Lee. 1988. "Spontaneous Order Analysis and Anthropology." *Cultural Dynamics* 1 (3):282–308.

_____. 1989a. "From Hunters to Herders: Subsistence Change as a Reproductive Strategy Among the Mukogodo." *Current Anthropology* 30 (2):224–234.

_____. 1989b. "Low Socioeconomic Status and Female-Biased Parental Investment: The Mukogodo Example." *American Anthropologist* 91 (2):414–429.

_____. 1989c. "Strings Attached." *The Sciences* 29 (3):2–4.

_____. 1990. "Family Trust." *The Sciences* 30 (6):10–12.

_____. 1991a. "Intention Versus Behaviour in Parental Sex Preferences Among the Mukogodo of Kenya." *Journal of Biosocial Science* 23:229–240.

_____. 1991b. "Preferential Parental Investment in Daughters Over Sons." *Human Nature* 2 (4):387–417.

_____. 1991c. "Wealth, Status, and Reproductive Success Among the Mukogodo of Kenya." *American Anthropologist* 93:345–360.

_____. 1992. "Old Dog, Old Tricks." *The Sciences* 32 (1):13–15.

_____. 1993. "Parental Favoritism Toward Daughters." *American Scientist* 81:272–279.

_____. 1994a. "Evolutionary Theories of Morality and the Manipulative Use of Signals." *Zygon: Journal of Religion and Science* 29 (1):81–101.

_____. 1994b. "The Use of Moralistic Statements in Social Manipulation: A Reply to Roy A. Rappaport." *Zygon: Journal of Religion and Science.* 29 (3):351–355.

_____. 1995. "Is There a Role for Culture in Human Behavioral Ecology?" *Evolution and Human Behavior* 16 (3):181–205.

_____. 1998. "Ethnographic Text Formation Processes." *Social Science Information/Information sur les Sciences Sociales* 37 (2):321–349.

_____. In press a. "Female-Biased Parental Investment and Growth Performance Among Mukogodo Children." In *Adaptation and Human Behavior: An Anthropological Perspective.* L. Cronk, N. Chagnon, and W. Irons, eds. Hawthorne, NY: Aldine de Gruyter.

_____. In press b. "Gethenian Nature, Human Nature, and the Nature of Reproduction: A Fantastic Flight Through Ethnographic Hyperspace." In *Biopoetics: Evolutionary Explorations in the Arts*. L. Brett Cooke and Frederick Turner, eds. New York: Paragon.

Dalrymple, G. Brent. 1991. *The Age of the Earth*. Stanford: Stanford University Press.

Daly, Martin, and Margo Wilson. 1983. *Sex, Evolution, and Behavior*. 2d edition. Belmont, CA: Wadsworth.

_____. 1988. *Homicide*. New York: Aldine de Gruyter.

Darwin, Charles. [1872] 1958. *The Origin of Species*. 2d ed. New York: Mentor.

D'Andrade, Roy G. 1992. "Schemas and Movitation." In *Human Motives and Cultural Models*. Roy G. D'Andrade and Claudia Strauss, eds. Cambridge: Cambridge University Press.

_____. 1995. "Moral Models in Anthropology." *Current Anthropology* 36 (3):399–408.

Davies, N. B. 1992. *Dunnock Behaviour and Social Evolution*. Oxford: Oxford University Press.

Dawkins, M., and T. Guilford. 1991. "The Corruption of Honest Signalling." *Animal Behaviour* 41:865–873.

Dawkins, Richard. 1976. *The Selfish Gene*. Oxford: Oxford University Press.

_____. 1995. *River Out of Eden*. New York: Basic.

Dawkins, Richard, and John Krebs. 1978. "Animal Signals: Information or Manipulation?" In *Behavioural Ecology: An Evolutionary Approach*. J. Krebs and N. Davies, eds., Oxford, UK: Blackwell Scientific.

Deaux, K., and R. Hanna. 1984. "Courtship in the Personals Column: The Influence of Gender and Sexual Orientation." *Sex Roles* 11:363–375.

Dedman, Penny. 1991. *Rites*. New York: Filmaker's Library. Videocassette.

DeFleur, M. L., and Frank R. Westie. 1958. "Verbal Attitudes and Overt Acts: An Experiment in the Salience of Attitudes." *American Sociological Review* 23:667–673. Reprinted in Deutscher, ed., 1973.

Dennett, Daniel. 1995. *Darwin's Dangerous Idea*. New York: Simon & Schuster.

Deutscher, Irwin. 1973. *What We Say/What We Do: Sentiments and Acts*. Glenview, IL: Scott, Foresman.

Deutscher, Irwin, Fred P. Pestello, and H. Frances G. Pestello. 1993. *Sentiments and Acts*. Hawthorne, NY: Aldine de Gruyter.

de Waal, Frans B. M. 1996. "The Biological Basis of Behavior." *Chronicle of Higher Education* 42 (40):B1–B2.

Dressler, A. 1989. "In the Grip of the Great Attractor." *The Sciences* 29 (5):28–34.

Dunbar, Robin. 1996. *Grooming, Gossip, and the Evolution of Language*. Cambridge: Harvard University Press.

Durham, William H. 1991. *Coevolution: Genes, Culture, and Human Diversity*. Stanford: Stanford University Press.

Durkheim, Emile. 1938. *Rules of Sociological Method.* Glencoe, IL: The Free Press.

Eaton, S. Boyd, Marjorie Shostak, and Melvin Konner. 1988. *The Paleolithic Prescription.* New York: Harper & Row.

Eddington, A. S. 1928. *The Nature of the Physical World.* New York: Macmillan.

Ekman, Paul. 1972. "Universals and Cultural Differences in Facial Expressions of Emotion." In *Nebraska Symposium on Motivation 1971.* James K. Cole, ed. Lincoln: University of Nebraska Press.

———. 1973. "Cross-Cultural Studies of Facial Expression." In *Darwin and Facial Expression: A Century of Research in Review.* Paul Ekman, ed. New York: Academic Press.

Ellis, Bruce J., and Donald Symons. 1990. "Sex Differences in Sexual Fantasy: An Evolutionary Psychological Approach." *Journal of Sex Research* 27:527–555.

Ember, Melvin and Carol R. Ember. 1990. *Anthropology.* 6th ed. Englewood Cliffs, NJ: Prentice-Hall.

Emlen, S. T., and P. H. Wrege. 1988. "The Role of Kinship in Helping Decisions Among White-Fronted Bee-Eaters." *Behavioral Ecology and Sociobiology* 23:305–315.

Ferraro, Gary, Wenda Trevathan, and Janet Levy. 1994. *Anthropology: An Applied Perspective.* Minneapolis: West.

Fisher, R. A. 1930. *The Genetical Theory of Natural Selection.* Oxford: Oxford University Press.

Frank, Robert H. 1988. *Passions Within Reason.* New York: W. W. Norton.

Freeman, Derek. 1982. *Margaret Mead and Samoa: The Making and Unmaking of an Anthropological Myth.* Cambridge: Harvard University Press.

———. 1989. "Fa'apua'a Fa'amū and Margaret Mead." *American Anthropologist* 91:1017–1022.

———. 1998. *The Fateful Hoaxing of Margaret Mead.* Boulder: Westview.

Fuller, C. J. 1976. *The Nayars Today.* Cambridge: Cambridge University Press.

Geertz, Clifford. 1973. *The Interpretation of Cultures.* New York: Basic.

Geertz, Clifford. 1988. *Works and Lives: The Anthropologist as Author.* Oxford: Polity Press.

Gewertz, Deborah. 1981. "A Historical Reconstruction of Female Dominance Among the Chambri of Papua New Guinea." *American Ethnologist* 8:94–106.

Gonzalez, Nancie. 1984. "Motion on *Science 83* Magazine." *Anthropology Newsletter* 25 (1):4–5.

Greenlees, I. A., and W. C. McGrew. 1994. "Sex and Age Differences in Preferences and Tactics of Mate Attraction: Analysis of Published Advertisements." *Ethology and Sociobiology* 15 (2):59–72.

Gross, Daniel R. 1992. *Discovering Anthropology.* Mountain View, CA: Mayfield.

Hamilton, W. D. 1964. "The Evolution of Social Behavior." *Journal of Theoretical Biology* 7:1–52.

Harpending, Henry. 1995. "Human Biological Diversity." *Evolutionary Anthropology* 4 (3):99–103.

Harpending, Henry and Renee Pennington. 1993. *The Structure of an African Pastoralist Community: Demography, History, and Ecology of the Ngamiland Herero.* Oxford: Clarendon.

Harpending, Henry, Alan Rogers, and Patricia Draper. 1987. "Human Sociobiology." *Yearbook of Physical Anthropology* 30:127–150.

Harris, Marvin. 1993. *Culture, People, Nature: An Introduction to General Anthropology.* New York: HarperCollins.

Haviland, William A. 1996. *Cultural Anthropology.* Fort Worth: Harcourt Brace College Publishers.

Hawkes, Kristen. 1983. "Kin Selection and Culture." *American Ethnologist* 10:345–363.

_____. 1990. "Why Do Men Hunt? Some Benefits for Risky Choices." In *Risk and Uncertainty in Tribal and Peasant Economies.* Elizabeth Cashdan, ed. Boulder: Westview.

_____. 1991. "Showing Off: Tests of Another Hypothesis About Men's Foraging Goals." *Ethology and Sociobiology* 11:29–54.

_____. 1993. "Why Hunter-Gatherers Work: An Ancient Version of the Problem of Public Goods." *Current Anthropology* 34 (4):341–361.

Hawkes, Kristen, Kim Hill, and James O'Connell. 1982. "Why Hunters Gather: Optimal Foraging and the Ache of Eastern Paraguay." *American Ethnologist* 9:379–398.

Hawkes, Kristen, and James O'Connell. 1983. "Affluent Hunters? Some Comments in Light of the Alyawara Case." *American Anthropologist* 83:622–626.

Hawkes, Kristen, James F. O'Connell, and Nicholas Blurton Jones. 1989. "Hardworking Hadza Grandmothers." In *Comparative Socioecology: The Behavioural Ecology of Mammals and Man.* V. Standen and R. Foley, eds. London: Blackwell.

Hawkes, Kristen et al. In press. "The Grandmother Hypothesis and Human Evolution." In *Adaptation and Human Behavior: An Anthropological Perspective.* L. Cronk, N. A. Chagnon, and W. Irons, eds., Hawthorne, NY: Aldine de Gruyter.

Hayek, F. A. 1955. *The Counter-Revolution of Science: Studies on the Abuse of Reason.* Glencoe, IL: The Free Press.

Heider, Karl. G. 1991. *The Grand Valley Dani, Peaceful Warriors.* Fort Worth: Harcourt Brace College Publishers.

Heimans, Frank. 1988. *Margaret Mead and Samoa.* Sydney: Cinetel Productions Ltd., the Australian Broadcasting Corporation, and the Discovery Channel. Published in New York by Brighton Video and Wombat Film and Video. For bibliographic details regarding the transcript for this videotape, see O'Meara 1988.

Hepper, Peter G., ed. 1991. *Kin Recognition.* Cambridge: Cambridge University Press.

Hicks, David, and Margaret A. Gwynne. 1994. *Cultural Anthropology.* New York: HarperCollins.

Hill, Kim, and Hillard Kaplan. 1988a. "Tradeoffs in Male and Female Reproductive Strategies Among the Ache: Part 1." In *Human Reproductive Behaviour: A Darwinian Perspective.* L. Betzig, M. Borgerhoff Mulder, and Paul Turke, eds. Cambridge: Cambridge University Press.

_____. 1988b. "Tradeoffs in Male and Female Reproductive Strategies Among the Ache: Part 2." In *Human Reproductive Behaviour: A Darwinian Perspective.* L. Betzig, M. Borgerhoff Mulder, and Paul Turke, eds. Cambridge: Cambridge University Press.

Howard, Michael C., and Janet Dunaif-Hattis. 1992. *Anthropology: Understanding Human Adaptation.* New York: HarperCollins.

Hrdy, Sarah Blaffer. 1990. "Sex Bias in Nature and in History: A Late 1980s Reexamination of the 'Biological Origins' Argument." *Yearbook of Physical Anthropology* 33:25–37.

Hume, David. [1739/40] 1966. *A Treatise of Human Nature, Volume II, Book III: Of Morals.* Reprint, Oxford: Oxford University Press.

Humphrey, Nicholas K. 1976. "The Social Function of Intellect." In *Growing Points in Ethology.* P. P. G. Bateson and R. A. Hinde, eds. Cambridge: Cambridge University Press. Reprinted in Byrne and Whiten, eds., 1988.

Ing, R., N. L. Petrakis, and J. H. C. Ho. 1977. "Unilateral Breast-Feeding and Breast Cancer." *Lancet* 2:124–127.

Ingold, Tim. 1994. "Humanity and animality." In *Companion Encyclopedia of Anthropology: Humanity, Culture and Social Life.* Tim Ingold, ed. London: Routledge.

Irons, William. 1979. "Cultural and Biological Success." In *Evolutionary Biology and Human Social Behavior: An Anthropological Perspective.* N. A. Chagnon and W. Irons, eds. North Scituate, MA: Duxbury.

_____. 1997. "Looking Back Two Decades." In *Human Nature: A Critical Reader.* Laura Betzig, ed. Cambridge: Cambridge University Press.

Johnson, Gary R. 1986. "Kin Selection, Socialization, and Patriotism: An Integrating Theory." *Politics and the Life Sciences* 4:127–154.

_____. 1987. "In the Name of the Fatherland: An Analysis of Kin Term Usage in Patriotic Speech and Literature." *International Political Science Review* 8:165–174.

_____. 1989. "The Role of Kin Recognition Mechanisms in Patriotic Socialization: Further Reflections." *Politics and the Life Sciences* 8:62–69.

Jolly, Alison. 1966. "Lemur Social Behaviour and Primate Intelligence." *Science* 153:501–506. Reprinted in Byrne and Whiten, eds., 1988.

Kagwa, Sir Apolo. 1934. *The Customs of the Baganda.* New York: Columbia University Press.

Kaplan, Hillard, and Kim Hill. 1985. "Hunting Ability and Reproductive Success Among Male Ache Foragers." *Current Anthropology* 26 (1):131–133.

Kassindja, Fauziya, Layli Miller Bashir, and Gini Kopecky. 1998. *Do They Hear You When You Cry*. New York: Delacorte.

Kauffman, Stuart. 1995. *At Home in the Universe*. Oxford: Oxford University Press.

Keesing, Roger M. 1974. "Theories of Culture." *Annual Review of Anthropology* 3:73–97.

Konner, Melvin, and Carol Worthman. 1980. "Nursing Frequency, Gonadal Function and Birth Spacing Among !Kung Hunter-Gatherers." *Science* 207:788–791.

Kottak, Conrad. 1994. *Cultural Anthropology*. New York: McGraw-Hill.

Kroeber, A. L., and Clyde Kluckhohn. 1952. *Culture: A Critical Review of Concepts and Definitions*. Cambridge, MA: Papers of the Peabody Museum of American Archaeology and Ethnology, Harvard University, volume 47, number 1.

Kroeber, Theodora. 1961. *Ishi in Two Worlds*. Berkeley: University of California Press.

Kuhn, Thomas. 1962. *The Structure of Scientific Revolutions*. Chicago: University of Chicago Press.

Kuper, Adam. 1992. "Post-Modernism, Cambridge and the Great Kalahari Debate." *Social Anthropology* 1:57–71.

Kuznar, Lawrence A. 1997. *Reclaiming a Scientific Anthropology*. Walnut Creek, CA: Altamira.

Lang, Daryl. 1998. *The Curse of a Thousand Chain Letters: An E-mail House of Horrors*. Web site. URL: http://chainletters.org.

LaPiere, R. T. 1934. "Attitudes vs. Actions." *Social Forces* 13:230–237. Reprinted in Deutscher, ed., 1973.

Layde, Peter M. et al. 1989. "The Independent Associations of Parity, Age at First Full Term Pregnancy, and Duration of Breastfeeding with the Risk of Breast Cancer." *Journal of Clinical Epidemiology* 42 (10):963–973.

Le Boeuf, B. J. 1974. "Male-Male Competition and Reproductive Success in Elephant Seals." *American Zoologist* 14:163–176.

Le Guin, Ursula K. 1969. *The Left Hand of Darkness*. New York: Ace.

Liebig, Justus. 1842. *Animal Chemistry, or, Organic Chemistry in Its Applications to Physiology and Pathology*. London: Taylor and Walton.

Liebow, Elliot. 1967. *Tally's Corner: A Study of Negro Streetcorner Men*. Boston: Little, Brown.

Lohman, J. D., and D. R. Reitzes. 1954. "Deliberately Organized Groups and Racial Behavior." *American Sociological Review* 19:342–348. Reprinted in Deutscher, ed., 1973.

Lowie, Robert. [1917] 1929. *Culture and Ethnology*. New York: Peter Smith.

Lumsden, Charles, and Edward O. Wilson. 1981. *Genes, Mind, and Culture*. Cambridge: Harvard University Press.

———. 1982. *Promethean Fire*. Cambridge: Harvard University Press.

Lynch, Aaron. 1996. *Thought Contagion*. New York: Basic.

Malotki, Ekkehart. 1983. *Hopi Time: A Linguistic Analysis of the Temporal Concepts of the Hopi Language*. Berlin, Germany: Mouton.

Mandelker, I. L. 1984. *Religion, Society, and Utopia in Nineteenth-Century America.* Amherst: The University of Massachusetts Press.

Marcus, George E., and Dick Cushman. 1982. "Ethnographies as Texts." *Annual Review of Anthropology* 11:25–69.

Marcus, George E., and Michael M. J. Fischer. 1986. *Anthropology as Cultural Critique: An Experimental Moment in the Human Sciences.* Chicago: University of Chicago Press.

Mayr, Ernst. 1961. "Cause and Effect in Biology." *Science* 134:1501–1506.

McFarland Symington, M. 1987. "Sex Ratio and Maternal Rank in Wild Spider Monkeys: When Daughters Disperse." *Behavioral Ecology and Sociobiology* 20:421–425.

Mead, Margaret. 1928. *Coming of Age in Samoa.* New York: William Morrow.

_____. 1935. *Sex and Temperament in Three Primitive Societies.* New York: William Morrow.

Menger, Carl. 1892. "On the Origin of Money." *Economic Journal* 2:239–255.

McGrew, William C. 1992. *Chimpanzee Material Culture.* Cambridge: Cambridge University Press.

Mills, C. Wright. 1940. "Methodological Consequences of the Sociology of Knowledge." *American Journal of Sociology* 46:316–330.

Miller, Tim. 1995. *How to Want What You Have: Discovering the Magic and Grandeur of Ordinary Existence.* New York: Henry Holt.

Moore, Alexander. 1992. *Cultural Anthropology: The Field Study of Human Beings.* San Diego, CA: Collegiate Press.

Moore, George Edward. 1903. *Principia Ethica.* Cambridge: Cambridge University Press.

Moore, Jerry D. 1997. *Visions of Culture.* Walnut Creek, CA: Altamira.

Moore, John H. 1990. "The Reproductive Success of Cheyenne War Chiefs: A Contrary Case to Chagnon's Yanomamö." *Current Anthropology* 31 (3): 322–330.

Moscucci, Ornella. 1990. *The Science of Woman: Gynaecology and Gender in England, 1800–1929.* Cambridge: Cambridge University Press.

Murdock, George Peter. 1967. *Ethnographic Atlas.* Pittsburgh: University of Pittsburgh Press.

Nanda, Serena, and Richard L. Warms. 1998. *Cultural Anthropology.* 6th ed. Belmont, CA: Wadsworth.

Nozick, Robert. 1974. *Anarchy, State, and Utopia.* New York: Basic.

O'Meara, J. T. 1988. "Post-Production Script of *Margaret Mead and Samoa* Videotape" (see Heimans 1988).

_____. 1989. "Anthropology as Empirical Science." *American Anthropologist* 91 (2):354–369.

_____. 1997. "Causation and the Struggle for a Science of Culture." *Current Anthropology* 38 (3):399–418.

Packer, C., D. A. Gilbert, A. E. Pusey, and S. J. O'Brien. 1991. "A Molecular Genetic Analysis of Kinship and Cooperation in African Lions." *Nature* 351:562–565.

Peacock, James L. 1986. *The Anthropological Lens: Harsh Light, Soft Focus.* Cambridge: Cambridge University Press.

Peoples, James, and Garrick Bailey. 1997. *Humanity: An Introduction to Cultural Anthropology.* Belmont, CA: West/Wadsworth.

Pérusse, Daniel. 1993. "Cultural and Biological Success in Industrial Societies." *Behavioral and Brain Sciences* 9:267–322.

Peyton, Kelly J. 1996. *Postpartum Depression in the Absence of Lactation: An Evolutionary Perspective.* Unpublished M.A. thesis, Department of Anthropology, Texas A&M University.

Pinker, Steven. 1994. *The Language Instinct.* New York: William Morrow.

_____. 1997. *How the Mind Works.* New York: W. W. Norton.

Pipher, Mary. 1996. *The Shelter of Each Other: Rebuilding Our Families.* New York: G. P. Putnam's Sons.

Popper, Karl. 1978. *Conjectures and Refutations.* London: Routledge & Kegan Paul.

Premack, D., and G. Woodruff. 1978. "Does the Chimpanzee Have a Theory of Mind?" *Behavioral and Brain Sciences* 1:515–526.

Pulliam, H. Ronald, and C. Dunford. 1980. *Programmed to Learn.* New York: Columbia University Press.

Rappaport, Roy A. 1968. *Pigs for the Ancestors: Ritual in the Ecology of a New Guinea People.* New Haven, CT: Yale University Press.

_____. 1994. "On the Evolution of Morality and Religion: A Response to Lee Cronk." *Zygon: Journal of Religion and Science* 29 (3):331–349.

Read, K. E. 1965. *The High Valley.* New York: Scribner's.

Reyna, S. P. 1994. "Literary Anthropology and the Case Against Science." *Man* 29:555–581.

Ridley, Matt. 1993. *The Red Queen: Sex and the Evolution of Human Nature.* New York: Macmillan.

_____. 1996. *The Origins of Virtue: Human Instincts and the Evolution of Cooperation.* New York: Viking.

Robbins, Richard H. 1997. *Cultural Anthropology: A Problem-Based Approach.* 2d ed. Itasca, IL: F. E. Peacock.

Rosaldo, Michelle Z. 1984. "Toward an Anthropology of Self and Feeling." In *Culture Theory: Essays on Mind, Self, and Emotion.* Richard A. Schweder and Robert A. LeVine, eds., Cambridge: Cambridge University Press.

Roscoe, J. 1911. *The Baganda: An Account of Their Native Customs and Beliefs.* London: Macmillan.

Rosenberg, Alexander. 1980. *Sociobiology and the Preemption of Social Science.* Baltimore: The Johns Hopkins University Press.

Rosenzweig, Mark R. 1979. "Responsiveness of Brain Size to Individual Experience: Behavioral and Evolutionary Implications." In *Development and Evolution of Brain Size: Behavioral Implications.* Martin E. Hahn, Craig Jenson, and Bruce C. Dudek, eds. New York: Academic.

Rosman, Abraham, and Paula G. Rubel. 1998. *The Tapestry of Culture: An Introduction to Cultural Anthropology.* 5th ed. New York: McGraw-Hill.

Russell, Bertrand. 1969. *Bertrand Russell Speaks His Mind.* New York: Bard.

Sahlins, Marshall. 1976. *The Use and Abuse of Biology.* Ann Arbor: University of Michigan Press.

Salmon, Catherine A. 1998. "The Evocative Nature of Kin Terminology in Political Rhetoric." *Politics and the Life Sciences* 17 (1):51–57.

Sanjek, Roger, ed. 1990. *Fieldnotes: The Makings of Anthropology.* Ithaca: Cornell University Press.

Sawyer, J., and R. A. LeVine. 1966. "Cultural Dimensions: A Factor Analysis of the World Ethnographic Sample." *American Anthropologist* 68:708–731.

Scheper-Hughes, Nancy. 1992. *Death Without Weeping.* Berkeley: University of California Press.

_____. 1995. "The Primacy of the Ethical: Propositions for a Militant Anthropology." *Current Anthropology* 36 (3):409–440.

Schiffer, Michael B. 1987. *Formation Processes of the Archaeological Record.* Albuquerque: University of New Mexico Press.

Schultz, Emily A., and Robert H. Lavenda. 1995. *Cultural Anthropology: A Perspective on the Human Condition.* 3d ed. Mountain View, CA: Mayfield.

Schusky, Ernest L. 1983. *Manual for Kinship Analysis.* 2d edition. Lanham, MD: University Press of America.

Scott, James C. 1985. *Weapons of the Weak: Everyday Forms of Peasant Resistance.* New Haven, CT: Yale University Press.

_____. 1990. *Domination and the Arts of Resistance: Hidden Transcripts.* New Haven, CT: Yale University Press.

Scupin, Raymond. 1992. *Cultural Anthropology: A Global Perspective.* Englewood Cliffs, NJ: Prentice-Hall.

Seuss, Dr. 1961. *The Sneetches and Other Stories.* New York: Random House.

Sforza, Teri. 1995. "Fertility Technology Virtually Unpoliced in US." *Orange County Register*, May 28. [From WWW, n.p.]

Sherman, P. W. 1977. "Nepotism and the Evolution of Alarm Calls." *Science* 197:1247–1253.

Silverman, Martin G. 1972. "Ambiguation and Disambiguation in Field Work." In *Crossing Cultural Boundaries: The Anthropological Experience.* Solon T. Kimball and James B. Watson, eds. San Francisco: Chandler.

Soltis, Joseph, Robert Boyd, and Peter J. Richerson. 1995. "Can Group-Functional Behaviors Evolve by Cultural Group Selection? An Empirical Test." *Current Anthropology* 36 (3):473–494.

Speke, J. H. 1864. *Journal of the Discovery of the Source of the Nile.* New York: Harper and Brothers.

Sperber, Dan. 1985. *On Anthropological Knowledge.* Cambridge: Cambridge University Press.

Spiro, Melford. 1984. "Some Reflections on Cultural Determinism and Relativism with Special Reference to Emotion and Reason." In *Culture Theory: Essays on Mind, Self, and Emotion.* Richard A. Shweder and Robert A. LeVine, eds. Cambridge: Cambridge University Press.

Stark, Rodney. 1996. *The Rise of Christianity.* Princeton, NJ: Princeton University Press.

Thiessen, Del, Robert K. Young, and Ramona Burroughs. 1993. "Lonely Hearts Advertisements Reflect Sexually Dimorphic Mating Strategies." *Ethology and Sociobiology* 14 (3):209–229.

Thornhill, Randy. 1981. *"Panorpa* (Mecoptera: Panorpidae) Scorpionflies: Systems for Understanding Resource-Defense Polygyny and Alternative Male Reproductive Efforts." *Annual Review of Ecology and Systematics* 12:355–386.

Tiger, Lionel. 1996. "My Life in the Human Nature Wars." *The Wilson Quarterly* 20 (1):14–25.

Tiger, Lionel, and J. Shepher. 1975. *Women in the Kibbutz.* New York: Harcourt Brace Jovanovich.

Tinbergen, Niko. 1963. "On Aims and Methods of Ethology." *Zeitschrift für Tierpsychologie* 20:410–433.

Tooby, John, and Leda Cosmides. 1992. "The Psychological Foundations of Culture." In *The Adapted Mind: Evolutionary Psychology and the Generation of Culture.* Jerome H. Barkow, Leda Cosmides, and John Tooby, eds. Oxford: Oxford University Press.

Townsend, J. M. 1989. "Mate Selection Criteria: A Pilot Study." *Ethology and Sociobiology* 10:241–253.

_____. 1993. "Sexuality and Partner Selection: Sex Differences Among College Students." *Ethology and Sociobiology* 14:305–330.

Townsend, J. M., and G. Levy. 1990a. "Effects of Potential Partners' Costume and Physical Attractiveness on Sexuality and Partner Selection." *Journal of Psychology* 124:371–389.

_____. 1990b. "Effects of Potential Partners' Physical Attractiveness and Socioeconomic Status on Sexuality and Partner Selection." *Archives of Sexual Behavior* 19:149–164.

Turke, Paul. 1989. "Evolution and the Demand for Children." *Population and Development Review* 15:61–90.

Tylor, E. B. 1871. *Primitive Culture.* London: J. Murray.

van den Berghe, Pierre. 1979. *Human Family Systems.* New York: Elsevier.

Vayda, Andrew P., Anthony Leeds, and David B. Smith. 1961. "The Place of Pigs in Melanesian Subsistence." In *Symposium: Patterns of Land Utilizations and Other*

Papers. Proceedings of the 1961 Annual Spring Meeting of the American Ethnological Society. Viola E. Garfield, ed. Seattle: University of Washington Press.

Vlassoff, M., & Vlassoff, C. 1980. "Old Age Security and the Utility of Children in Rural India." *Population Studies* 34:487–499.

Vonnegut, Kurt. 1976. *Slapstick, or Lonesome No More!* New York: Delacorte Press.

Warriner, C. K. 1958. "The Nature and Functions of Official Morality." *American Journal of Sociology* 64:165–168. Reprinted in Deutscher, ed., 1973.

Weinberg, Steven. 1992. *Dreams of a Final Theory.* New York: Pantheon.

Whiteford, Michael B. and John Friedl. 1992. *The Human Portrait: Introduction to Cultural Anthropology.* Englewood Cliffs, NJ: Prentice-Hall.

Wiederman, Michael W. 1993. "Evolved Gender Differences in Mate Preferences: Evidence from Personal Advertisements." *Ethology and Sociobiology* 14 (5):331–351.

Williams, George C. 1983. *Adaptation and Natural Selection.* Princeton, NJ: Princeton University Press.

———. 1992. *Natural Selection: Domains, Levels, and Challenges.* New York: Oxford University Press.

Williams, T. 1884. *Fiji and the Fijians.* London: Hodder and Stoughton.

Wilson, D. S., and E. Sober. 1994. "Reintroducing Group Selection to the Human Behavioral Sciences." *Behavioral and Brain Sciences* 17:585–654.

Wilson, Edward O. 1975. *Sociobiology: The New Synthesis.* Cambridge: Harvard University Press.

———. 1998. *Consilience: Unity of Knowledge.* New York: Knopf.

Wolf, Margery. 1992. *A Thrice-Told Tale: Feminism, Postmodernism, and Ethnographic Responsibility.* Stanford: Stanford University Press.

Womack, Mari. 1998. *Being Human: An Introduction to Cultural Anthropology.* Upper Saddle River, NJ: Prentice-Hall.

Woolfenden, G. E., and J. W. Fitzpatrick. 1984. *The Florida Scrub Jay: Demography of a Cooperative-Breeding Bird.* Princeton, NJ: Princeton University Press.

Wrangham, Richard W. et al., eds. 1994. *Chimpanzee Cultures.* Cambridge: Harvard University Press in cooperation with the Chicago Academy of Sciences.

Wright, Robert. 1994. *The Moral Animal: The New Science of Evolutionary Psychology.* New York: Pantheon.

Wynne-Edwards, V. C. 1962. *Animal Dispersion in Relation to Social Behaviour.* Edinburgh and London: Oliver and Boyd.

Zahavi, Amotz, Avishag Zahavi, Naama Zahavi-Ely and Melvin Patrick Ely. 1997. *The Handicap Principle.* Oxford: Oxford University Press.

Index